The
Midas
Touch

The World's Leading Experts Reveal Their Top Secrets to Winning Big in Business & Life

FEATURING

Joe Vitale

& Leading Experts From Around The World

The Midas Touch
The World's Leading Experts Reveal Their Top Secrets to
Winning Big in Business and Life

ISBN-13: 978-0-9912964-9-1
ISBN-10: 0991296494

Published by: Expert Author Publishing
http://expertauthorpublishing.com

Canadian Address:
1265 Charter Hill Drive
Coquitlam, BC V3E 1P1
Phone: (604) 941-3041
Fax: (604) 944-7993

US Address:
1300 Boblett Street
Unit A-218
Blaine, WA 98230
Phone: (866) 492-6623
Fax: (250) 493-6603

Contents

The Secret Few Know
Dr. Joe Vitale

"Couldn't you just buy it off the shelf?"

I was trying to tell my youngest brother about a cholesterol lowering natural health product I had invested in, called Ideal Cardio Formula. I explained that I spent $12,000 on it so I could personally have it to use myself.

He didn't understand.

"Couldn't you just buy the key ingredients of the formula in separate bottles and then take *that*?" he asked. "It would have cost you far less."

He was thinking like most people think. He was trying to save a buck and take care of himself. In his mind, the "buy the basic ingredients" approach was smart thinking. It was efficient and frugal. From that limited perspective, he was right.

But he was missing a secret few people know.

He was missing the Midas Touch to success. I figured he could make $100,000 or more if he knew this secret, so I proceeded to explain it to him.

"Look, when my doctor said I had high cholesterol," I began, "I wanted a solution without taking his prescribed drug, which I knew had potential dangerous side effects. So I went to a friend of mine who is also a medical doctor, but with an interest in handling health problems with herbs first."

"I understand *that*," my brother said.

"Let me continue," I said. "My herb-loving doctor told me he had a formula that he developed himself that was a blend of twelve ingredients that he guaranteed would lower cholesterol in thirty days. I naturally wanted it."

"I would, too," he said.

"But he said he didn't have any of the product, and added it would take twelve thousand dollars to make a batch of about two thousand bottles of it as a minimum run from a manufacturer."

"Two thousand bottles!" my brother exclaimed. "Again, couldn't you just get the list of ingredients and then go to a health store and buy the ingredients and take *those*?" he asked. "You wouldn't have to spend twelve grand!"

My brother was making the mistake most people do. He was thinking of only himself. As long as he did, he wouldn't have the "Midas Touch" for success.

I saw this moment as a prime chance to transform his life forever – if he'd just listen to me. I wasn't going to give up.

"If you don't mind, let me give you a lesson in prosperity," I continued. "You're right. I *could* buy the ingredients in separate bottles, spend a hundred bucks, and lower my cholesterol. I'd be doing a smart thing. I'd be taking care of myself. But the *smarter* approach would be to take care of others *and* myself."

He still didn't get it.

"By investing twelve grand in 2,000 bottles of the cholesterol lowering material, I'd become an entrepreneur who changes lives. How many people need to lower their cholesterol? Millions? I could sell those extra bottles to those other people. I just went from taking care of just me to taking care of others – and being rewarded with money!"

I still don't think he understood.

But this is the secret few know.

Most people don't think beyond themselves. That's fine for survival. You *do* need to take care of yourself. But the real secret to success is when you take care of others *and* yourself.

I'm really talking about a shift in perception. You might think that this is a mental operation that you'll never be able to do. It might seem like a foreign way of perceiving the world around you.

I used to believe I couldn't think like this, too. I remember thirty years ago listening to marketing genius Jay Abraham say he'd walk into a gym and see a hundred ways they could make more money. He'd then rattle them off. I'd listen to him and say to myself, "How do you think like that?"

But there have been clues along the way.

When I was doing research for my book on P.T. Barnum, the great circus promoter who I later wrote about in *There's A Customer Born Every Minute,* I was baffled to learn that he could see what others could not.

For example, when he heard of a little boy who would never grow over three feet tall, people told Barnum that it was sad. But when Barnum met the little boy, his eyes saw "Super Star!"

Barnum transformed that little boy into the man the entire world loved and paid to see: General Tom Thumb.

I marveled that Barnum had the Midas Touch for seeing gold in what others saw as nothing special.

But today I *do* think like that.

How did I go from poverty thinker to Midas Touch thinker?

By reading books, listening to audios, going to events, and retraining my brain.

Now I can't turn off the Midas Thinker. Now it looks around and sees opportunities everywhere.

In my book, *Attract Money Now,* I say one of the seven steps to financial freedom is to think like an entrepreneur.

How do you think like an entrepreneur?

By hearing your doctor say you need to lower your cholesterol, and then realizing others might need to do so too. As you discover your own solution, you turn that solution into a product others will buy.

Win- win.

Here's another example to help you integrate this Midas Touch way of thinking:

A decade or so ago, a young woman wrote to me, asking questions about making money online. I met with her and listened to her story.

She talked about her life, her interests, her hobbies and so forth. She actually didn't believe people could really make money online, and certainly doubted her own ability to do so.

But as I listened, I heard an opportunity.

She mentioned she had taught herself how to play the guitar in a weekend.

"A weekend?" I asked, a little in disbelief myself. At the time, I was an aspiring musician. (Today I have six albums out.) I wanted to know more.

"I created a basic method that let me play popular songs without much effort," she said, completely clueless to the goldmine she was sitting on.

"Can you teach others to play guitar in a weekend?" I asked.

She said she could.

I then encouraged her to write an eBook on her method. That came as a surprise to her. She never thought of it before. She didn't know how to write an eBook, but I told her lots of how-to manuals are available, including the one I coauthored with Jim Edwards, *How to Write and Publish Your Own EBook – in only 7 days!*

She went on to write her eBook, put up a site, and start selling it. To her amazement – as she didn't think the idea would actually work – she started making sales.

But the story gets even better.

She was a struggling college student. She was borrowing money from her parents. With the eBook selling, she had cash coming in. A little at first. But then more. One of the people who bought her product, and loved it, offered to buy the rights to her eBook – for ten thousand dollars!

For this broke college student, it was like winning the lottery.

But it wasn't from the lotto.

It was from "Midas Touch" Thinking!

Here's one final example for you:

Years ago I was interviewed about my audio program (*The Abundance Paradigm*) while in Chicago recording it. The host asked, "Joe, with the economy in the tank and sinking, what are we to do?"

"How do you know it's sinking?" I asked. "Where did you hear about it?"

He seemed surprised by my questions. But I didn't give him a chance to reply. I went on saying – "The only reason you think it's terrible out there is because you are being programmed to think so by the mainstream media."

The host stared at me as I went on my soapbox and continued –

"The media is trained to find bad news and broadcast it to you. The more they do it and you believe it, the worst the world looks. It then becomes a self-fulfilling prophecy. You live from the new paradigm of scarcity and the media, doing its job, broadcasts it. You don't even see it happening. It feels real. You take it as reality."

At that point I could have told the true story of how ABC News came to my home – twice – and interviewed me for hours. They even filmed an entire evening with me and celebrity fitness model Jennifer Nicole Lee during one of my private masterminds.

Six months later all that footage was edited down to barely three minutes of highly distorted "news." The same news station that broadcast a slimy angle about my work also broadcast commercials for drugs with known side effects, such as death.

That's mainstream news.

You might call it the Scarcity Network.

The Scarcity Network typically airs facts in negative terms and slants. For example, a reader sent me the following –

"Joe, just a further example for you of negative news. The US originally thought that we lost 131,000 jobs in July, it is actually 77K jobs better and it is still packaged as bad news. Then, some people feel that their job prospects are better so they decide to enter the labor force and we show an uptick in unemployment. Wouldn't a headline of: "US retains 77,000 more jobs than originally thought while more workers choose to enter the labor force" be a better headline?"

Yes, it would be a better headline. But the Scarcity Network won't broadcast that. It's not the programming they want you to have in your head. They need you to live in fear. They need you controlled. They're not doing this out of any intentional conspiracy, but because they were programmed, too. This is their paradigm.

But I didn't relate either of the above to my interviewer. Instead, I turned direction and said –

"But what if there was a different channel to watch or listen to? What if there was an Abundance Network and all it broadcast were inspiring stories of people succeeding, accomplishing, attracting and achieving? What if they spun everything in a *good* way?"

I continued with –

"We all know that there are people doing well in the world right now. If this alternative media broadcast their positive news, and that's all you watched, you would soon be programmed to see the world as an abundant place. You would then create a self-fulfilling prophecy of abundance. You would then see abundance. You would then see opportunities. You would live in a world of miracles. *That* would then feel real."

At point I could have related the true story of the man who gave out credit cards to a handful of homeless people as a test to see what they would do with them. In every case, the homeless person used the card as they said they would, didn't misuse it to buy drugs or alcohol, and even returned the card when done.

The Abundance Network would report this story to show the hope and responsibility in the destitute; the Scarcity Network would run a similar test but air what didn't work, even if they had to make it up, or they would complain that the cards had low limits, etc. They would find a weakness in an otherwise inspiring story. But they would focus on the weakness not to correct it but to communicate the unspoken programming, "See, told you homeless people were unreliable and its hopeless to try to help them!"

Back to my interview.

My host barely had time to stutter before I kept going with –

"Look. Both types of world exist right now — the lousy economy one as well as the abundant economy one. I'm not denying that. But it's like an optical illusion. Depending on how you look, the image is either an old woman, or a young woman. Reality itself is neutral. The question is, which view are you going to let program you? Which do you want to live in?"

I'm not aware of an Abundance Network yet. But until something like it exists, what are you to do?

Here's my suggestion –

Reprogram your mind.

Take charge of it.

Feed it the positive and you'll see and then attract the positive.

You'll "tune in" to the Abundance Network in your own mind. You'll have a paradigm shift (a shift of your view of the world) and you'll see abundance where you didn't before. It's basic Law of Attraction at work: you attract what you expect and believe. Just change the channel in your mind.

And then you can thumb your nose at the doomsayers out there.

You can become immune to them.

You can see reality as the grand optical illusion and choose which view of it best suits you.

It's your move.

And your mind.

Choose wisely.

Again, you can learn how to think like this. Read books on creativity, on marketing, on success. As you do, you will be programming your mind to think differently. This is possible for everyone, as the new science of neuroplasticity proves. You can literally retrain your brain.

And when you do, you will be living the secret few know – and prospering with The Midas Touch!

Dr. Joe Vitale, known globally as "Mr. Fire!", is the legendary bestselling author of numerous books, from Zero Limits to The Attracter Factor, and a standout star in the hit movie, The Secret. He has recorded many bestselling audio programs, such as The Missing Secret and The Secret to Attracting Money. He's an Internet pioneer, a Hypnotic Copywriter, and a Law of Attraction expert. He's also a musician. Once homeless, he now helps people worldwide with his Miracles Coaching program. His popular main site is www.JoeVitale.com Read his free eBook, Attract Money Now, at www.AttractMoneyNow.com

The Master Key To Unlocking Your Potential For Greatness & Abundance

Dan Lok

Most of us are familiar with the fable of King Midas. Despite his wealth, he believed that the only path to happiness was by accumulating even greater riches. He was obsessed with gold, and upon gaining favor with Dionysus, the God of wine and revelry, was granted one wish. As we know, he made the wish that everything he touched would turn to gold.

Of course, this turned out to be quite a curse for King Midas. Although he was able to add to his vast wealth by creating more gold with a mere touch, he couldn't enjoy holding flowers, eating his favorite foods, or even hugging his daughter because those things would instantly turn to gold. Despite his growing wealth he was thoroughly unfulfilled, until he convinced Dionysus to remove the "power." Having had the experience of limitless wealth, but the inability to enjoy any other part of his life, taught King Midas an important lesson and made him a much more generous person going forward.

Some people, like Midas, define success in terms of wealth. Others, learn or intuitively know, that abundance comes in many forms. The Midas Touch is about living a life that's filled with passion, joy, and purpose.

* * *

What makes some people's lives different from others?

Why is it that some people are more fulfilled and successful than others, and achieve great things in life, even though they might have started out life with nothing and had setbacks that should have doomed them to failure?

And yet there are others who have been given everything in life, but who rarely achieve personal fulfillment or success.

What is it that makes certain individuals so much more capable than others? Why are some people luckier than others? Who are those people who seem have "The Midas Touch" and succeed in almost anything? How exactly do the world's most prominent individuals seem to hit home run after home run?

In my life, I have had privilege of witnessing some pretty amazing things. I have seen people who have lost everything be inspired by a story, a quote, a picture, and as a result bounce back to the very top.

I have witnessed immigrants who barely spoke English start their own businesses and become financially independent in less than a few years. But nothing I have seen is more amazing to me than the power of the human mind and its evolution when given a purpose.

I am no psychologist, and am certainly not a scientist. I flunked my biology class, and was a C student in high school. In fact, I dropped out of college due to complete boredom.

I could start by telling you about my lifestyle or the possessions I accumulated, and how all that should make you buy into the message. But if I did, that by itself would go against the essence of my important message.

What I will tell you, however, is that the lifestyle I live today is the exact one I want to be living, not the one my initial circumstances had intended for me. The possessions I have today are not a good representation of how I wish to be remembered, and they certainly hold very little relevance to who I have become.

Something was different for me compared to when I was growing up. I am now more aware and conscious of what's going on around me. I saw most of life though a weird third-party lens, like a spectator. I liked to ponder, reflect, think and ask questions. From a very young age, I liked to observe my surroundings and those in it, while never really understanding at the time how everything and everyone was interconnected.

The most fascinating thing to me was that no matter what I did – like going on that dream vacation, starting a business, dating beautiful women – I never really found fulfillment; just temporary satisfaction. I bought new cars, homes, and luxury stuff that many people dream of, but I got bored with all of those things within a few months, sometimes a few days.

But there was ONE constant that didn't bore me. That was the knowledge gained from each experience. Regardless of the experience, whether positive or negative, I immediately absorbed that knowledge. I discovered that I had a natural talent for understanding, condensing and simplifying those experiences, and sharing those insights in a charismatic and profound way – a way that inspired others to take action. With each person I helped or touched I became more motivated, and I was full of energy to do it again and again.

At first, I believed that my own purpose was found, and it was helping others succeed and fulfill their own dreams and aspirations… BUT I WAS WRONG. I had not uncovered my purpose, but rather what my passion is.

This realization led me to dig deeper and ask myself more profound questions, and to look back at all my experiences, so I could understand what my purpose really was.

I asked myself over and over again, "How was I actually help-ing people? Was it changes to their mindset? Was it motivation? Was it inspiration? Was it business strategies? Was it marketing? Or perhaps was it nothing more than a kick in the butt when they needed it?"

I really couldn't tell what it was exactly that I was doing to help them. I knew I was helping them because their results changes (more revenue, higher income, more freedom, more free time, less stress, etc.). This proved that my method worked, even though it wasn't much more than various components of different things all coming together through my words, and presented in a way that everyone would understand.

That's when I realized that what I was teaching people was nothing more than a combination of my experiences. I also real-ized that how I was teaching them was exactly that way I wished to be taught.

However, WHY I was teaching them was because I wanted them to know what it's like to find their purpose. I wanted them to know what it's like to KNOW why you are here on earth and the importance that realization holds.

I was talking to a lady yesterday who is a serial procrastinator, filled with negative thoughts and who declared feelings of purpose-lessness in life.

I observed that purpose is ultimately found in action, not in philosophy alone. You can think, think, think all day long, but you can't build anything (including a life) without action to express your values. This lady spends a lot of time thinking about how she isn't good enough and how her actions wouldn't matter anyway, so she avoids taking any action.

The self-help industries claim that we each have one perfect reason for existing; that we need to lock ourselves in a room until we find it. And that once we do, everything will make sense and we can finally be fulfilled...

Why Trying To Discover Your Purpose Doesn't Work

The idea of a purpose probably came about as the agnostic's attempt at spirituality. One of the reasons that religion is so effective is because it has meaning and purpose built in. It's comforting to think that we are here for a reason.

When we tell people that they need a purpose in order to be fulfilled, it makes them feel empty until they have found it. That's why it's such a pervasive myth in the self-improvement industry (and why it's also such an effective marketing strategy).

Trying to "find our purpose out there" does not work because in some subtle way we are giving away our power to some mysterious force that is meant to supply us with what we yearn for.

But it is the very act of giving away our power that prevents us from leading a more meaningful life.

Telling someone that there is only one perfect thing that they were put on this earth to do is like telling them that there is only one perfect person for them, and then asking them to fall in love before the first date.

There is NO ONE perfect thing. There is only the best thing right now.

Instead of finding our purpose out there, it is our own responsibility to give purpose to our life, no matter whether our life is difficult or easy at the moment.

There are multiple studies showing that trying too hard to be happy can actually make us unhappy. I see the same thing happening with people trying to find their purpose. The searching just makes us feel worse.

Think about the times when you felt most purposeful.

If you are like most people, these were times when you felt you made a positive contribution to someone else or it was a time when you had a learning experience that helped you to understand the world more deeply.

In other words, most of us find the deepest sense of purpose through developing love and wisdom.

The good news is that developing love and wisdom can be done anytime and anywhere. We do not need to have that special project, recognition or fame to find a sense of purpose.

Instead, we can simply focus on questions like, "What can I learn from this situation?" and "How can I add value in this situation?"

As soon as we take these questions seriously and allow them to affect our inner being, a sense of purpose will arise even in the most difficult situations.

The very process of finding the answers to these sometimes difficult questions will give us a sense of heartfelt meaning. If we then act on these answers, the other circumstances of our life will also start to transform.

This is the way to find deepest satisfaction and one's life's purpose.

Purpose is the reason of your journey. I believe that if you follow your heart and live your purpose, the money WILL follow.

NOTE: If you don't know me, I'm Dan Lok. Husband, mentor & serial entrepreneur...
If you're an entrepreneur, let's you and I connect at http://www.danlok.com

One of The Most Important, But Often Overlooked, Strategies of Business Success!

DJ Richoux

My goal is for you to take one powerful but often overlooked concept and apply it your business or your professional practice or your career today.

Many business owners focus all their time, energy and resources on constantly growing their business – on increasing their gross sales month over month, quarter over quarter, or year over year. They become obsessed on always increasing sales and become blind to other aspects of their business.

Don't get me wrong. Growing your business and making more sales is important. However, your number one focus needs to be on making your business more profitable. Too many people focus on growth and not on profitability. This is a mistake.

One of the most efficient ways to make you more profitable is to focus on **selling and adding high-value products or services**

which have high gross profits. Selling more products or services or increasing gross sales doesn't automatically make you more profitable. In some cases it can cause you to go broke. Not all sales are equal. I am going to show you that some sales are worth ten times more to you than other sales.

One of the most common business lies people believe is you can make it up in volume. I am sure you have heard **"don't worry… you will make it up in volume"**. Truth be told, when margins are already tight you will never make it up on volume. Too many businesses are already running on gross profits of 10 to 30%, which are too low.

Price Does Matter

On a normal day Joanne, a health food store owner, sells 10 bottles of Vitamin C for $10.00 each with a gross profit of 30%. Joanne is thinking about cutting the price by 10% to $9.00 hoping she will make it up "in volume". What Joanne doesn't realize is to maintain her daily gross profit of $30 she would have to sell 50% more Vitamin C bottles every day, or 15 bottles a day.

By Joanne dropping her price by only 10% she is actually dropping her gross profit by 33%. Joanne is better off leaving her price at $10 and selling 10% less per day and only selling 9 units. When someone says you can make it up volume, don't believe them, you now know the facts and numbers.

How can Joanne increase her gross profits other than trying to increase her volume? I have a client who owns a small independent pharmacy, and we asked him the same question.

Actually, we asked a more powerful question, "What are at least 10 ways we can increase gross profits in 30 days or less without doing more advertising, bringing in more inventory or adding additional staff?"

We discovered that the pharmacy hadn't increased its dispensing fee in a long time to keep up with inflation, increasing employee costs and other variable costs. A typical pharmacy charges a dispensing fee to prepare a client's prescription. All we did was increase the dispensing fee by $1.00.

Do you think a dollar make can make a difference to gross profits? On a typical day my client will fill 100 prescriptions. That is an additional $100 in gross profit per day. For comparison's sake, if he was selling vitamin C like the health food store we discussed above, he would have to sell an additional 33 bottles of vitamins to make $99 more in gross profit per day. Do you think it is easier to fill 100 prescriptions at a slightly higher price, or sell an additional 33 bottles of Vitamin C each and every day?

That little one dollar is almost 100% gross profit. There are no additional costs of goods, advertising, inventory, or employee costs. Each one of those additional dollars can go right to the bottom line as net profit. $100 additional gross profit per day based on a five day week is $500 of additional gross profit per week, and based on a four week month is an additional $2,000 gross profit per month. Small numbers can make a big difference if you know what you are doing. **This is an amazing powerful concept.**

"But, My Business Is Different!"

Many business owners tell me I don't understand their business, their market or their competition. They say their business is different – they can't just increase their prices or margins. They say it is just too competitive, that they will lose clients. What they are really telling me is that they compete on price alone; that their product or service is just a commodity.

Trying to be the lowest price in your market is a weak strategy, especially for a small business. There will always be someone willing to sell lower then you. Even Wal-Mart, the low price leader, is feeling pressure from Amazon.com. Amazon is selling many products at prices lower then Wal-Mart. No one wins in this battle.

Competing on price alone is a bad strategy. Every business has tough competition and has to compete with multiple businesses in their local business area as well with online competitors. For example, my client the pharmacy owner competes against national chain stores, big box stores in his area, as well as online pharmacies.

My client is smart; he doesn't compete on price as he knows he can't win that war. He differentiates himself and competes on customer service and other factors. His pharmacy is known as the friendly pharmacy, because he makes it a point for his team to be very friendly and know their customers by first name. He guarantees their prescription will be filled in 15 minutes or less or the client doesn't pay the dispensing fee. There is always a pharmacist available to consult with, to ask any questions about taking multiple prescriptions and possible side effects or any other concerns a client may have. Smart business owners compete on factors they can win, and they are handsomely rewarded with additional profits.

Random Discounting Can Be Dangerous

I have another client that sells a coaching program. When you join his program you get program materials explaining his entire system. He usually charges $997 for this part of the program. He got into the bad habit of discounting the $997 down to $697 if you joined his program today.

What he didn't realize is how much this "one time discount" was affecting his gross profit. Let's say he sells 10 programs a month. 10 times 300 is $3,000. Three thousand dollars didn't sound like that much to him. He said, "that is the cost of growing my business and getting more clients." I told him that while there certainly is a cost to growing your business, he was paying a prince's ransom for that growth.

What he didn't understand is that not every dollar that comes into your business is equal. Discounting that $300 was washing gross profit down the drain. Gross profit is sacred to any business. There are no additional costs when you sell the program materials at their regular price of $997 instead of $697. Each time he sells a package, the additional $300 would go straight to the bottom line as net profit.

Discounting like this is the cousin to the **"don't worry… you will make it up in volume."** This one is **"don't worry… I will make it up from the client later."** You never do.

There Is a Better Way

Now, I have a challenge for you. Over the next 10 days look through all your products and services and choose one where you can increase the price without increasing your costs. Remember the powerful question, "What are at least 10 ways we can increase gross profits in 30 days or less, without doing more advertising, bringing in more inventory or adding additional staff?" Brainstorm with your business partners, your friends and your family. You will be amazed with what you will discover.

There is a better way. With a little creativity, planning and courage you can sell high value and high profit products and clients to your clients and your clients will love you for it!

I invite you to send me an email to **dj@djrichoux.com** with what you discovered doing this challenge, what you learned and how you increased your gross profits.

DJ Richoux is known as the "Profit Maximizer". Since 2001 he has been helping business owners maximize their profits in minimum time using simple and highly effective strategies. He has an unique ability of adding additional revenue streams to a business that most entrepreneurs don't realize exist. www.djrichoux.com

The THINK Solution™ The Five Keys to Unlocking the Life You Dream Of

Tom Barber and Sandra Westland

What if you could find the keys that would reveal to you the life you want? What if you could unlock your own secrets to your health, wealth and happiness and make your dreams become reality?

Living the life you desire and experiencing each day feeling free is easier than you think, but first you need to know how to rid yourself of all that is holding you back.

Over many years we have worked with people, as therapists, trainers and presenters around the world, hearing stories of people's struggles and frustrations with themselves and their lives. Be it feeling stressed, burnt out, depressed, anxious or just frustrated with life. From them, we have learned what holds people back and how to change this, taking intention into action, implementation and beyond. In our experiences, five key areas emerged that are essential to permanent life-changing personal growth, to help you get the life you want.

It *is* possible to attain the health you deserve so you can live a long and able life. It *is* possible to attain wealth, not only in terms of financial success, but also in a wealth of knowledge, love, relationships and spiritual connection. Once you enjoy feeling connected to the world, others and your own life, happiness comes in waves of abundance and your dream life becomes a reality.

So why doesn't everybody find these keys? Why aren't the secrets to this life of health, wealth and happiness freely available to all human beings? Well, probably the biggest secret of all is that they are! You just need to know how to find them.

The keys to living a life of true wonderment are available for each and every one of us, but you have to be genuinely ready to reach out and take them, and then you have to experience the know-how. All that you want to be, do, and have is waiting for you. It is right there for the taking, as it is for every human being.

In our research, our one-to-one therapy work and our training roles we have found that the five keys of our existence give us either the freedom to live our lives fully or to become the dumping ground of our dreams, where we get lost, held back from all that we can be. Whether this happens is often the result of experiences from your past, through fears that you've learned, or from the traumas you have faced. You will have your own unique story and valid reasons for being unhappy with where your life is at now.

However, in aligning yourself back into these five key areas with clarity and purpose, amazing and life changing things can and do happen. Once you unlock and liberate these areas of your life you can break out, move into your dreams, and claim what is rightfully yours – the freedom to be you and to live the life you want.

So, let's find out what these keys to a full and abundant life are.

Key Number 1 ~ TIME ~ Your Time is NOW!

How you exist with time is more of a Key to your success than you could ever imagine right now.

Being stuck in the past, making decisions and planning your future making sure something painful never happens again, means you are living your life looking in the rear view mirror. Being focused on the future, always towards a specific goal, where speed is of the essence, means there is little room for error, keeping you fixed and rigid in what you are doing, unable to open up to your creativity. Living from moment to moment means you are constantly firefighting, either yourself or what life throws at you, always seemingly in a crises or a drama. All are exhausting, relentless and holding you back.

In all of these you are missing out on the vitality of feeling alive and connected with the world and those around you ... you are not in the Now ... here is where your creative intuition lives, and where your potential and possibilities exist.

Do you remember a time when you weren't ruled by time? Maybe you recall the long lazy summer days of your youth, where time seemed to last so much longer than it does now, and even then you had the feeling that time was in abundance and you had forever. Your past seemed so close to you and the future was firmly in your grasp and you were truly present in the now. Imagine regaining that sense back in your life. How much calmer, clear-headed and productive would you be?

Gaining a balanced sense of time, so the past, the present and the future are of equal value, enables you to learn from what has been, live in the now and plan for the future, more easily than you could ever imagine. This opens up a place where there is more than enough time to get and enjoy the life you want.

Let's go further.

Key Number 2 ~ HOPE ~ Direct, Determine and Develop Your True Purpose.

Do you find yourself repetitively moving between hoping things will be different and despairing that nothing's changing? Have you ever hoped that a new fad diet would finally make the difference? Or hoped that someone would offer you that dream job, the one you've been waiting for? Perhaps you've hoped that your luck would simply one day change? Only to find that everything stays the same and life feels like you are on a treadmill? If so, then you are operating from the wrong kind of hope.

When you are connected with the state of hope that can move you to bigger things, *mature* hope, then you experience the kind of hope that is captivating, real, sustainable, and can never fail you. One that nourishes your spirit and motivates you to become the person you want to be, where you know exactly what you really want and why, and how to make it happen.

In this place there's no more wishing, wanting, or praying for change. No more procrastination, holding back or hiding behind "luck" or false and wishful hope. When you have this essential Key you will be able to stride forward in life decisively, with purpose and meaning, confidently on your intended mission!

A person with *mature* hope can wait. Patience becomes part of the plan because in this place you have wisdom! Mature hope is based on meaning and an appreciation of possibilities and that things are worthwhile, regardless of how they turn out. The process is the journey, and the journey is what nourishes, satisfies and validates your mission and gives you the health, wealth and happiness that you deserve.

Key Number 3 ~ IDENTITY ~ The Power of All of You - Claim Your True Identity

Your identity is not fixed… you are constantly gaining from new learnings as you live your life, but maybe deep inside you know you are holding yourself back. You are not being truly "you." So who you are needs expanding upon, to be experienced and most importantly owned. Have you noticed people who "fit" in themselves and how natural and confident they are? It's like they are "whole."

You can have this too! This is about putting "you" all together; bodily, psychologically and socially for lifelong liberation. Too much of one aspect of you (the social animal) and not enough of another (health and fitness) leads to inner conflicts, procrastination and outcomes you don't want in your life.

Imagine no longer wondering who you are or feeling like you are unfulfilled or not reaching your true potential. Imagine connecting with and owning who you truly are, creating inner balance, peace and comfort in your own skin *and* having as much energy as you could ever need, and then even more! It's possible when you really get to know who "you" are.

Key Number 4 ~ NEUROLOGY ~ Activate, Illuminate and Liberate Your Personal Power

Modern research demonstrates that your brain continuously creates new neural pathways, can adapt existing ones and re-engage unused ones. So change, physiologically, is a *truth*, but how can you do this to get the life you want?

Firstly you create the pathway and then, to carve the much needed groove, you need neurological conditioning. This requires maximum powerful sensory input, as you need to engage all of your senses, so that your new success "programs" that you want to operate from, become embedded in your brain and new synapses start connectively firing automatically. Then the new experiences of you become real, genuine and felt. This enables you to *feel* your power and *know* that you are becoming a force to be reckoned with.

Your brain has so much untapped potential – it just needs

activating and reconditioning and then you will feel you are firing from all cylinders.

Key Number 5 ~ KNOWING ~ Celebrate What Can Never Now Be Unknown

Really *knowing* how you are moving into your inner transformation, within both your body and mind, without any doubt to what changes are unfolding, is the last Key to feeling settled and natural with how your future will be.

Have you ever been so completely sure about something that nothing, absolutely nothing, will change your mind? You just know that what you believe is 100% right. Nothing could convince you otherwise. *This* is knowing!

In embedding this powerful embodied sense of knowing – you just feel it throughout your body and mind – you'll never be able to "un-know" what you will now know. Try now this very moment to forget the most important person or thing in your life. You just can't do it, can you? That's because the most important things in your life are stored not just in your memory but throughout the whole of you – in every cell, molecule and atom of your being. Think of a parent's love for their child. It doesn't need explaining does it? It holds its own weight. It carries its own power. You just manage it, care for it and be the bearer of its importance.

With this knowing you can go forward, transformed, empowered to live your life as *you* choose, invigorated with passion, purpose and meaning. Now is your time to live the life you have dreamed of.

These five keys take you to living the life you really want, transformed to being the real you. The THINK Solution™ is the process that shows you how and takes your dreams and turns them into reality. It is a fascinating journey to the freedom of taking control of your life.

The mission? For you to become fully empowered with the clarity to make your life one long lasting fulfilling experience, with the desire to act and make things happen … starting from the moment you choose, and you have to choose, as this is the deal.

Are you ready?

About Tom and Sandra

Tom Barber and Sandra Westland are co-founders of The THINK Solution™. They have been teaching, coaching and mentoring people all over the world with transformational change strategies since the early 1990's. Their extensive doctoral research in areas such as emotion and the human body continue to enrich and enhance their work.

Through their journey, they have unearthed the essential keys that help people gain freedom from within, and developed them into key programs that help people to eradicate life challenges and problems, for brighter, richer, healthier and more abundant lives.

You can begin your own journey of transformation now with your free "Breakthrough CD", and other powerful tools that will excite you to make the changes you desire at www.theTHINKsolution.com

Offerings:
The Miraculous Power
of A Simple Gesture
Christopher Barrett

We live in a technology-filled world where one may be under the assumption that we are more connected than ever. However, all one has to do is leave the comfort of their home to discover this is less than true... all one has to do is look up from their screen to not recognize their surroundings, to crash into another vehicle or find themselves in uncomfortable silence with those around them. Being present is a "thing" of the past... and that "thing" is an offering! The offering of being present for one another, engaging in conversation, sharing a smile, a thought, a story, and sharing love!

Offerings can be found throughout history. Religious and spiritual texts are filled with mention of them. Offerings can range from lighting candles, a simple flower in a bowl, incense, prayer, song- chants, fire, spirit plates, dance, to saying grace before meals – all with the intention of creating a greater connection to the Divine. Nature herself runs on the natural flow of offerings, and without it she would not exist. The flower offers nectar to the bee, and the bee offers pollination to the plant. Without the bee, this world would cease to exist.

You came with your own purpose and gifts to share; your own Midas Touch. As St. Francis so eloquently put it, "Remember when you leave this earth you can take with you nothing that you have received. Only what you have given; a heart enriched by honest service, love sacrifice and courage.

Anything that we give as an offering (including anything emotional, physical, spiritual or monetary) has a vast and profound impact to the known and the unknown. Offerings can be positive or negative. For instance, are you offering someone a compliment or a criticism? A blessing or a judgment? Forgiveness or a grievance? How can we expect to manifest that which we desire if the time away from manifesting intentions is burdened with negativity?

Everything we do extends energy out, including our words. We hear many times over that we "reap what we sow" and our "words and thoughts create our reality."

But how do we know they are received? Our offerings are always received, whether we know it or not. Perhaps that smile you gave to a stranger was just what the stranger was praying for. Perhaps when you lead with a giving heart you answer prayers that you are unaware of.

This happened to me.

One morning, about 18 years ago, I was awakened by a knock-on the door. I was greeted by two policemen who asked me if I wanted to call someone. Not knowing the horror I was about to be introduced to, I shrugged off the question and denied their offering.

The next few minutes were met with a cloud of emotions that burned deeply into my heart. My best friend had been brutally murdered. I tried to wrap my mind around the how and why.

The officers were on a mission to discover who would have cause to harm my friend. They gave me some time to compose and invited me to later stop by the station.

Running strictly on adrenaline I did my best to gather my thoughts and breathe. Not really with any known intention of what to do next, I jumped in my car and drove to the nearest florist.

I asked them to create a bouquet with every yellow flower they had. Why yellow? I hardly knew what I was doing, but yellow represented emotional healing to me, and all I could think was that my friend's last moments were spent alone and in terror. So yellow would indeed be perfect.

With the arrangement in hand, I went to her house that was now crawling with law enforcement and one of the officers obliged my request and placed the flowers on her front stoop.

In matters like these one finds themselves searching for answers where they may not have looked before. So lucky me, having a friend who is a world-renowned psychic who frequently works with police.

Hoping that she would be able to shed some light on this I went immediately to her house. What came next altered me for life. The first information she shared was that she was in contact with my friend. She further described her in the presence of two other loved ones that had also departed recently. But the most amazing thing of all came next. She told me that my friend was saying "thank you" to me, and that my friend was holding a huge bouquet of yellow flowers.

To say that I could have been knocked over by a feather is an understatement, as I had made no mention to anyone about the flowers.

In that room I was given irrefutable proof that even the most ambiguous offerings are received, and that we are all indeed connected by something far greater than our mere humanness or material items. There is a sacred thread that runs through all things.

Even though I had been taught this truth as a child, I now held in my heart a deep knowing. A knowing that would change every future intention and experience, and would be part of my teachings. We are all indeed one. What we do to one, we do to all.

Our words and actions carry energy that leaks out to all we touch. Imagine for a moment that if the "offerings" have such an impact on the intangible, what impact your offerings have on the tangible.

If in being more mindful of each breath, discerning of each and every thought, word and action, in between manifesting what you desire, you were to offer love to every experience, you would then discover yourself immersed in a sea of miracles.

So why would you want to implement a life around offerings? Is it not said that giving of oneself returns tenfold? Giving is the energetic key to open the doors of creation. When we offer kindness to others we set off a chemical reaction that generates more peace and happiness. So what would your offering be? Remember that even a simple gesture of forgiveness, gratitude or love can change another's life in ways we may never know. But we know that in doing so it is indeed received. Live knowing what you're offering is gold. And all that you touch will then surely turn to gold.

Ready to move through life's roadblocks? Visit Christopher at naturesinterpreter.com for more information on how she can help you carve an easy path to swiftly move thru those roadblocks and live your truest purpose.

Christopher Barrett, is a heart based intuitive Life Coach trained by shamans since she was a child. A survivor of two near-death experiences, she is gifted with a unique perspective. A non-denominational minister with a master's in dream psychology, and a pending doctorate, she has more than 30 certifications in various arenas of healing modalities, including specialties in conscious relationships and communication, addictions, grief counseling, and animal connection and communication, and signs in nature.

The Power is Already Within You

JP Beaudoin

What do you do when you are told you have less than six months to live? My aortic valve was collapsing on itself. Genetics and a life of extreme consumption – a real rock and roll lifestyle filled with food, drugs, and alcohol – had brought me to this point. I had a choice. I could continue to die a slow death or I could follow doctor's orders and have surgery.

September 11th, 2013: I lay on the table in the operating room. The surgery was scheduled to last three hours. Complications during surgery meant I spent nine hours in surgery and 26 under anesthesia. During this time I had what can only be described as an "out of body" experience.

I could see myself on the table. Floating in the upper corner of the room, I felt in perfect control. A sense of serenity and energy flowed through me. I knew that everything was okay and I could sense a beautiful power and peace filling me. Where you might expect fear (after all it's strange to see yourself lying on an operating table), I felt calm. I knew then that there was a superior power or energy.

Does it Take a Near Death Experience to Realize True Power?

Life changes a bit when you learn that you might die. You realize what's important and you assess your life. It happens almost instantaneously, almost without consciousness. Your body and mind have to make a decision. Give in or fight.

When I learned that I had a heart problem that might kill me, I decide to fight. We're not talking about the kind of fight that makes you feel tough and powerful, but rather the type of fight that glows with faith and positivity.

I asked the universe to let me live and start my life anew. As part of that request I began to immediately face everything with a positive attitude. The people around me found it bizarre that I was so positive and living like nothing was happening – like I wasn't facing a life-altering surgery.

Life After Surgery

Everything has changed. I am living a very different life now. I am always happy and grateful for every breath. I've always been aware of the Law of Attraction on some level. My father taught me about the power of the subconscious. And yet it took a near death experience to bring it all back to me – to remind me of the power that we all have within us.

Things and Events Don't Happen To Us, They Happen For Us.

What if the things that happen in your life don't happen to you, rather they happen for you? There's a big difference, and it changes the way you approach the world. What if the surgery and the life or death decision that I had to make happened <u>for</u> me?

Think about what's happening in your life right now? Imagine it's not happening to you, but for you. How does that change your perspective?

After my surgery, I asked the Universe for a hotel in Costa Rica.

I have always dreamed of owning a hotel in Costa Rica. I wanted to create a multi-functional center that served creative people like artists and musicians, as well as allowing others to experience their own unique types of personal growth, all within an unbelievable country. I didn't have the cash flow to buy the hotel. I asked the Universe to find me the way to buy a hotel that I had visited a couple of months before; one I thought could be the perfect venue for my dream.

Rather than feeling like my lack of cash flow happened to me, I embraced it as something that happened for me. I talked to the hotel owner and it all came together as if guided by the hand of the Universe, which of course it was. I was able to get the hotel without any deposit or cash down.

It is my most sincere belief that my poor health, which led to my new way of seeing life because of the experience I had to go through, and my beliefs in the power of the subconscious, also led me to my dream life. And here's the great opportunity for you. You don't have to wait for a life or death situation for you to realize your power and start living your dream life.

The Three Conditions to Receiving

There are three basics condition to receive what you want in life.

1. **Work On Your Subconscious** – Every day, before going to sleep and before getting out of bed, spend 15 to 30 minutes repeating affirmations, meditating and becoming aware of your subconscious thoughts. Before you can control your thoughts, you need to become aware of them.

2. **Shift Your Focus** – There are three factors that influence your emotions. First you've got to focus; focus on what you want in life in a positive way. Second, watch your language. Use a positive and creative language when you speak to

yourself and to others. Third, pay attention to your body. Get connected to it. Walk, breathe and move like a winner and believe in your power.

3. **Ask for What You Want**

Whatever the mind can conceive and believe, the mind can achieve. ~Napoleon Hill

---

With your subconscious properly conditioned, and a shift in your thoughts and actions so that you are focused on the positive, you can ask whatever you want and you will receive it. There's an art and a skill to asking for what you want.

1. Be specific. Get very clear and focus on what you want.

2. Be clear about the why. Why do you want that?

3. Believe that what you want is coming to you, be certain, have the faith and act as it is. Feel it.

4. Be excited about what you want. Celebrate!

5. Visualize your life as if you already have achieved it.

6. Take action, be committed, and create momentum.

7. Be thankful. Have a sense of gratitude to be able to say thank you to the universe.

It's not magic. Realizing your true power and creating the life you want takes work. You have the strength within you. Put yourself in the good state, and live your life in gratitude and positivity. Remember thoughts become things.

JP Beaudoin lives in beautiful Quebec, Canada and in Costa Rica. He's the owner of multiple businesses where he focuses on creating outstanding and memorable lifetime experiences for his clients. He's a Certified Life & Business Strategies, personal Coach and a Law of Attraction Practitioner. Receive a free 30 minute intervention-coaching session at www.jpbeaudoin.com.

Reclaim the Extraordinary Magic of Birthing

Ilona Brown

I t's time for the world to acknowledge that the birth experience itself is equally as important as birthing a healthy baby.

As a mother of two, Lactation Consultant, Doula and Childbirth educator, my philosophy is to give an expectant mother all the information and support possible to empower her to make her own choices, whether that is natural birth, epidural or even a planned cesarean.

My job is to paint the picture of what's possible.

I still remember feeling dumbfounded in the first classes I took almost ten years ago. Why would anyone actually choose to have a natural birth? It never occurred to me that there could be something more about the experience. The more I learned, read, attended birth conferences, and watched positive videos of women in labor (such as home births or the famous "Orgasmic Birth" or

Rikki Lake's "The Business of Being Born"), the more I began to see things in a different light.

I realized it wasn't *new* information I needed to acquire as much as *forgetting all the negative messages I'd been receiving* since I was a little girl.

Becoming pregnant with my first son Max coincided with teaching childbirth education at my local hospital and attending births. Slowly, the feelings of fear and anxiety were replaced with anticipation, confidence and immense curiosity.

I began to see birth as offering access to an exciting spiritual journey; one that is accessed when you see yourself meeting and overcoming your edge time and again, pushing forward when you don't think you can anymore. Trusting your body's inner wisdom. Trusting your partner and doctor/midwife to help guide you… Meeting your baby for the very first time.

And now dear reader, I must ask you:

WHAT IF you thought of childbirth as a romantic, intimate experience that has the potential to bring you and your partner closer than ever?

OR

AS a profound opportunity to explore unchartered spiritual and emotional depths within yourself?

Imagine you are going on your honeymoon. You can travel there in coach or first class. The drive over can be smooth or bumpy. Eventually you get where you want to go, but the journey is a HUGE part of the experience.

It's the same with childbirth. Why not give yourself a first class birth experience?

Set the scene: soft lights, warm bubble bath, scented candles lit around the bedroom, soft music playing in the background and dim lights…

Yes! The same conditions that lead to a beautiful and romantic evening (what got the baby in) are the ideal conditions to give birth (help the baby out)!

This cocoon-like setting, along with techniques like aromatherapy, sounding and a supportive birth partner, offers the opportunity to enter the meditative, non-thinking portion of the brain. Accessing this "primitive" part of the brain is what allows mom to fully surrender to the birth process.

Labor Mind

Labor offers the *one and only* opportunity to experience your body's highest levels of oxytocin it will ever produce! When the right environment is cultivated, labor can be a meditative, transcendent experience.

Think about when you are in a very intimate setting, about to have sex. The hormones start working their magic. Inhibitions are let go of and you "lose yourself."

You have tapped into the reptilian side of the brain; the instinctual, feeling, NON-thinking part of the mind.

This is the same state of mind you want to re-create when in labor. You want that primal side to come out from hiding, and the logical, thinking part of the brain to recede into the background.

It can be a truly awesome experience to fully surrender to the process; to go into the unknown full of wonder and curiosity, and emerge out the other side a fuller, deeper person.

This is just one reason why so many women want to experience a natural birth. (Other reasons include the safety and wellness of both mama and baby, but for now we will focus on the emotional value of birthing.)

On a side note: Does this mean that a mother must have a natural birth to experience the wonder and excitement described above? No! It is possible to have a cesarean birth, to ask for an epidural or other help and still experience all these things to some degree.

With the right preparation, information and support team you can significantly increase your chances for a normal, un-medicated birth.

So many women birth their child and then feel depressed, even though they have a normal, healthy baby.

Why?!

Many times the reason is because she did not feel that her birth experience was valued. When a mother feels that she was honored in the birth experience as much as the care of having a healthy baby, she feels very differently, even if things may go along a different route than planned.

Meet the Romeo of all Hormones: Oxytocin

Birth is the time when your body will produce its highest-ever amount of the feel-good hormone oxytocin. It is the feel-good hormone that helps you bond with friends and loved ones, and it is present in large quantities during enjoyable sex. This is why men and women (especially women) develop such close bonds with the people we give ourselves to in this way.

In all its wisdom, nature gave us oxytocin to help us cope with the challenge of labor, bond with our baby and encourage milk production.

Your body weeps the tears your eyes don't shed." Author unknown.

There is a profound mind-body connection in pregnancy and birth. To increase your chances for a healthy pregnancy and birth, deal with your demons; your mother issues, father issues, fears and dreams. You are about to become a parent. Of course this brings up tremendous emotion! The more honest you are with yourself, **the easier your labor will be.**

Now is the time to examine your beliefs around birth.

Did you grow up on a farm watching cows and horses give birth? Did your mom have a great home birth experience? Or is the opposite true... perhaps she had a cesarean and felt unsupported? Pay attention to the messages you've been receiving your entire life. They play a role in your subconscious and conscious mind. Better to deal with these things now, BEFORE you are in labor.

Techniques like hypnotherapy can help you to retrain your mind on the subconscious level (which is the true motivator for 99% of what we do).

The name of the game is not to have an un-medicated birth at all cost. It's about letting the woman decide what is best for her.

I have found that the best support typically comes from a mid-wife in a hospital, a birth center or a home birth. However there are many doctors out there who also support the normal birth process (affectionately called MD's – Midwife in Disguise!)

THIS NEXT THING I WILL SAY IS CRITICAL:

The key is to know which questions to ask before choosing your birth professional. How do you know ones to ask? As a consultant I often work with clients to help them understand the key questions they must ask their birth professional *in their first trimester of pregnancy*. Yes, you can ask later, but asking the right questions early on in the process ensures that you are with the right birth professional, and sets the tone throughout pregnancy.

The more honest you are with yourself and the people around you, the better your experience will be. In its infinite wisdom, your body knows if you are holding something back.

So often a mom is worried about her partner or other family member, not wanting to hurt feelings. But in labor, having some-one that you are not fully comfortable with can actually slow your cervix from opening.

Being surrounded by people you feel you can be yourself fully with has the effect of helping your cervix to open and the birth to be more joyful; and yes, even be experienced as less painful.

And if you do decide to have an epidural, or it turns out that medical intervention was appropriate, good for you! Own it! You knew what you needed at the right time and used your voice to ask for it.

Be thankful that help was available; be proud of your choices and don't fall into an unnecessary guilt trip.

Giving birth is an experience that will test you heart, mind, body and soul. You will have learned something valuable about your own physical and emotional strength.

The total honesty, vulnerability and strength you just experienced will lead you to understand why I call this a profound exploration into your spiritual growth.

You will be transformed forever.

ILona's passion for maternity and baby care, combined with extensive training as a Lactation Consultant, Childbirth Educator, and Birth and Postpartum Doula, render her uniquely skilled to soothe, motivate, inform and prepare clients for their labor experience. Visit www.lamotherhood. com to schedule a private consult, access prenatal meditation cds, books, healing aromatherapy and more.

Creating Momentum
Eric Bunn

L ike many in the world today, I've been searching for the secret to real happiness. For me, that involves expanding my ability to overcome new challenges while having fun. After college I was at a major crossroads in my life. I knew there had to be something better than the rat race. This prompted years of massive soul searching and a hunger to understand the most successful and happiest people. One reoccurring theme I noticed in their lives was momentum, which coincided with their most significant accomplishments and experiences. I have isolated some key elements and constantly apply these tools in my life.

Inspiration

Over the past several years, I've been more aware of inspiration in my life, or being In-Spirit. I have learned much about intentions and manifesting desires. For example, in 2014 I received an email from a well-known self-improvement author about using intentions to easily acquire a new car. I had just purchased my first new car 16 months prior and was very happy with it. I noted the email but took little action. The next week I took my car in to get some expensive physical damage fixed. While waiting, I met a representative for the dealership. She found me eligible for a special retention program that qualified me for the newest version of my car with full sports package. For almost the same monthly cost I could avoid any damage expenses and high mileage on my used car by trading it in. I attracted a new car almost without even trying.

This showed me the power of intentions and motivation to not miss future opportunities. Unfortunately, these moments can slip away if we don't act upon them. I feel like I'm at the beginning stages of mastering this process, and finally at the point where I am creating lasting momentum. I've noticed many get a little taste of success and don't maintain it. Limiting beliefs, negative thoughts, and life often get in the way.

Setup for Success

Plan Success: I've found most successful people never rely on luck, and redefine luck to mean being prepared for an opportunity. Ben Franklin said, "If you fail to plan, you plan to fail." We need to write out our plan. Brian Tracy said, "A genius without a road map will get lost in any country." I've heard that many of the greatest authors write the last chapter of a story first so they know how it ends, and then just fill in the details.

Find Your Mentor: Once an intention is decided we should copy someone who is achieving it successfully. We can use their successes and mistakes as a manual. When possible, ask them for personal guidance. Successful people often find joy in helping someone else succeed.

Circle of Influence: It's been said we are an average of the five people we hang out with the most. Surrounding ourselves with positive people builds our circle of influence. It's easier to stay on target when you're influenced by supportive people.

Don't Procrastinate

Once we receive inspiration, we must act quickly. It's human nature to wait for the conditions to be perfect before taking action. The best time to start is now. Momentum isn't created or maintained while we think about it. In many success stories, the individual just started doing, and all the help they needed magically appeared.

Many of us overthink a situation. For me, I often have fear of starting if I don't know every detail, or fear of continuing if the plan isn't going perfectly. That's called paralysis by analysis. Henry Ford said, "Whether you think you can, or think you can't, you're right."

Sometimes we don't feel like moving into action because we are in a bad mood or just flat out tired. We have to make a conscious effort to take some action and do something towards our goal every single day. Taking the action can literally give us the energy we need, or put us in the mood we originally desired. I've practiced this first hand. Next time you don't feel like moving forward, I challenge you to take Nike's recommendation and "Just do it!"

Laser Focus

Sometimes our momentum is slowed down because we get sidetracked. It's not enough to just take action. We must focus. In my own life, I have a major goal that I have not sold out to yet. I had created some momentum towards achieving it, but got offered an exciting opportunity and took it. It allowed me to use similar skill sets, but promised quicker results. I learned and profited, but ultimately it derailed the momentum of my larger vision. My written plan and circle of influence corrected me and now I truly appreciate the necessity of focus.

Never Quit

Like Yoda said, "There is no try, only Do or Do not." If you stop or even pause, your mind can create negative thoughts that lead to doubt, and momentum dies. Imagine you roll a huge boulder up a mountain and get 90% to the top. Then you decided to rest while just propping the boulder up. As you strain to hold it, you get fatigued and when you try to start again, it's too difficult to put the boulder in motion. You can see the finish but you've lost the momentum, so doubt starts to snowball in your mind and now that boulder is rolling right back to the beginning.

Invite momentum into your life, find your inspiration, set up your success system, take action, and stay focused! In the latest Rocky movie he tells his son, "You, me, or nobody is gonna hit as hard as life. But it ain't about how hard you hit. It's about how hard you can get hit and keep moving forward; how much you can take and keep moving forward. That's how winning is done!" Whether you're just beginning your journey or starting anew, momentum is a powerful key to rewarding and lasting success.

Eric Bunn is an entrepreneur, athlete and idealist. He graduated from the University of Pennsylvania, home of Wharton, and started on the 1998 Ivy League Championship football team. Eric has 15 years of success in business and developing sales teams. To learn more about Eric's newest project, go to ericbunn.acndirect.com

Finding One's Path
Marko Buric

I was born in Slovenia as a long-wanted only child into a quite complicated family. Because of this, my mother was over-protective towards me, and I would often get my way. However, my education was quite strict and I was not spoiled in the same way as many other only children were. At the age of 5, we relocated to Switzerland. I had to learn a totally different language, find new friends, and go to a different school…

My father always wanted me to outperform, therefore what I did was never good enough. Subconsciously I wanted his approval, his confirmation that I am worth of being loved, so I always wanted to do my best. This led to my perfectionism, which almost made me insane, as I was putting so much effort and getting no results. When I was 16, we returned to Slovenia, and I tried to adapt once more. I lived my normal student (and later on professional) life, gathered working experiences, met with friends, enjoyed doing sports. I also had a couple of relationships, but for one or another reason they wouldn't work, and I always wound up getting hurt. I came across some texts by Louise L. Hay, and I liked them, but they didn't really hit me. It wasn't the right time…

When I met the woman who would become my wife, we started our relationship based on honesty, mutual respect and a wish for making it work. We had our ups and downs, but we managed to talk about most of what was bothering us. She was the first person who accepted me for what I was. She explained me that I deserved love, regardless of my education or profession. As I solved one issue after another, I dug deeper and discovered more limiting beliefs and issues that prevented me from having the life I wanted. I tried to solve them by myself, but wasn't particularly successful. Asking for help is difficult for many people, and so it was for me.

Three years ago I moved with my wife back to Switzerland, and recreated my life. I thought I would be able to deal with issues alone, but I had to hit a low point before I was able to start looking for help. I experienced it as being unhappy with my life; feeling no purpose or joy. I lost all interest in everything. Truth be told, I had everything a person could want. I had a good job and I had good money. I had a great wife and was successful, but felt like life was so difficult and complicated. I was unhappy and I didn't know why. Something was not matching, and it was puzzling me.

So I started looking for answers. My path to a better life started like so many others. It began with books. Again I stumbled upon Louise L. Hay, was led to Rhonda Byrne, whose books pointed towards Joe Vitale. His books, and his coaching program performed by Dr. Janeen J. Detrick, helped me to understand what was going on and how to change the path I was on. I was able to recognize and deal with my emotions, my way of thinking and my life approach in general.

Letting Go of a Common Limiting Belief

Removing limiting beliefs for me was one of the necessary steps to change my patterns and to start creating my ideal life. My coach, Dr. Janeen J. Detrick, helped me overcome two key hurdles that kept me from moving forward. The first hurdle was a limiting belief that many people can relate to; money. I had a scarcity mindset. I said things like "there's never enough money." Although I actually had enough to cover all my needs and more, I felt the financial responsibility as a burden and was afraid of a sudden event that could wipe out all my savings. In a way, I was afraid of the future.

I was always looking after the money, checking on how much I had and how much things cost. I was stressed about paying invoices, getting the salary, buying goods or services. I was always planning and thinking in advance how to allocate the money I had. This is why I had difficulties when deciding to buy my coaching. Fortunately, I was at the point in my life where I knew I was on the right path and that I had to do something different if I wanted different results. I went for it and never looked back. This is how I met Janeen, my great coach, who helped me to find and understand my limiting beliefs, and of course to choose the right path, method and affirmation to clear them.

Calming the Monkey Mind

I had what I learned through coaching to call a "monkey mind." It's when you cannot control your thoughts and they jump from idea to idea without focus or awareness. They can be positive or negative, but they won't let you have your inner peace. Through practices like meditation, deep breathing and other techniques I learned from my coaching, I began to work on it. I learned to calm my mind, to give my thoughts a certain direction, to become the film director of my thinking. My most recent achievement is that I learned to lower my blood pressure.

The Path is Often Unexpected

As a result of coaching and learning about the Law of Attraction, I changed my mindset and began to see new opportunities that before were invisible to me. This led me to take some unexpected steps in my career, like the decision to start with a 3-year part-time study, in addition to my work. One day after class we headed to a bar to study and talk. After we'd done our work for school, my classmate's mom invited us for a drink with her friends. When we sat down she introduced me her personal life coach.

I was shocked to say the least – I didn't know such a thing existed. Then I realized I'd found my calling. I can share what I've learned and help people move, develop themselves and change what they don't like in their lives. I accepted the "mission" that I can share my life lessons, also in form of friendly advices, because people don't always ask for help when they need it. But after my initial excitement, I got scared of this path when thinking of what I'd have to do, how I'd have to plan and... so part of me wanted to forget the whole idea of being a coach.

Just a couple of days after expressing that, I had a conversation with a person I've never met before explaining some of what I've learned through coaching, and she called me her "guru." Again, I was shocked. I realized that sometimes the path chooses you, and not the opposite.

This message of sharing what I know and what I've learned continues all the time. As I was sorting through my goals, beliefs, and lessons I was also creating a project management manual for work. The two ideas came together and I was advised to write a book, or to write a contribution to it.

Writing a book was never on my radar and yet the opportunity wouldn't go away. I began receiving emails, letters, and having conversations that all directed me toward writing this chapter. So an inspiration or your path is... going to keep poking at you until you follow it.

I know my path is to share my lessons and techniques with others, and that writing this chapter is only the beginning. The start was however, my own wish to change the circumstances or to change me, to find answers, the insight and new ideas from authors, coaches, friends and family. If I hadn't done that, I wouldn't be where I am today.

Don't Wait to Ask for Help

If you are not able to resolve your issues alone, you don't have to wait until you're depressed, sad, unhappy or facing illness, just reach out and get another perspective, insight or guidance from others. You are worth of a better life today. If you look close enough, the signs are all around you. They will help you uncover the next step towards your personal fulfillment.

A short time ago I was having dinner with colleagues after a meeting. We left the meeting and headed to the parking lot. It was storming. I was in the car with one of my colleagues and we were waiting for the others because my boss asked me to wait as they didn't knew where to go. Seconds later a large tree was ripped from the ground. It fell just a few meters from my car. If I'd been driving towards to the parking exit, it would have hit my car. It missed everyone and left us with a strong reminder to be grateful for every breath and to seize the moment. Today is the day that you have, so why waste it being miserable? You want to be happy, this is the ultimate goal, so why not ask for help, look for guidance and start living a better life today.

As a result of what I have learned through my growth and progression, I will be able to help you identify YOUR limiting beliefs and also lift you into experiencing a paradigm shift that will clear those blocks! Contact me at http://www.markoburic.com or write at ma.buric@gmail.com

---

Marko Buric was born in Nov. 1979 in Slovenia. After changing countries and jobs, he now lives with his wife in Switzerland. He is currently working in IT Security, studying business informatics and preparing himself for a new path of being a life coach.

The Playground
Brigitte Carignan

I feel my heart pound. My breathing is getting faster. The muscles in my legs are getting warm; they're burning. It feels great. I count the stairs one at a time, focused on my goal. I'm headed up five floors. Endorphins are flowing and I'm enjoying the amazing power of my body.

I'll repeat this exercise several times today. It's now part of my routine. I walk up and down the stairs during my coffee break and my lunch. It's a priority. Regardless of how busy the day is, I make time. It keeps me calm, centered, and able to stay in a positive mindset. My workplace is an opportunity to help me to be in a better shape. I feel grateful about my working environment. It's my playground.

Yes you read it right, my workplace is my playground – why not?

Why not get up each day and go to work with the mindset of going to play? I am a nurse and my playground is the hospital that I work in.

It wasn't always this way. Working in the hospital used to make me miserable.

I was convinced that my work environment was the source of my unhappiness. I felt overworked and underappreciated. Working as a nurse in Quebec means that you're overloaded with patients to care for. My life was working, sleeping, and eating. I had no social life, with the exception of complaining about the job with other nurses. I blamed my unhappiness on my work and I was willing to tell anyone who asked just how awful my job was.

Deciding that I might be happier working somewhere else, I took a leave of absence from the hospital. I stayed in nursing but moved to another area. The complaints and negativity continued. I still wasn't happy at work.

I decided that I must have chosen the wrong career. I felt stuck. Financially, I couldn't make a job change. At 40 years old I felt dramatically alone. Although I was surrounded by family I was so mired in unhappiness that I couldn't see the blessings around me.

Not sure where to go or how to solve my happiness problem, I took a leap of faith. It was a small one. I went with someone to their numerologist appointment. He gave me a consultation on the spot, without an appointment and told me that I was beginning a new cycle in my life. I was going to feel happier and have a more rewarding personal and professional life. He went on to explain that I would feel introspective. "This is a year of big change," he said. "You will open your eyes to who you are and what you want to do with your life."

I felt relieved, and a little bit excited. Maybe I'd find a solution. He introduced me the Ho' Oponopono tool. It took another small leap of faith to give it a try really, I felt like I didn't have anything to lose.

The clearing that happened with Ho' Oponopono began creating awareness inside of me. I remember a physic sciences class teacher that gave grades based on improvement. If your test scores improved, he gave you a higher grade on your report card. He didn't average them like most teachers, but rather rewarded by considering the process individually. He taught me to approach problems with an open mind. I'd forgotten about this teacher until that day I'd met the numerologist. He used to write on the board, $E \geq mc^2$.

His message was that energy is more powerful than we imagine. Be open to it, he said. Driving home that day, I decided to be open-minded to living in another way. What I was doing clearly wasn't working. I need to change my mindset and how I approached not only my job, but also my life.

I'd be lying if I said it was instantaneous and easy. I had to learn how to shift my mindset. The book, *Zero Limits*, and the movie, The Secret, helped get, and keep, me on track.

Consequently, I decide to visualise a better environment at work. I visualized myself with more energy and less stress. I visualized time during the day to breathe and shifts that ended on time. I visualized easier patients and a happier life. Gradually, it became easier to get up and go to work with a smile on my face and gratitude in my heart. Instead of dreading the day, I allowed myself to see how beautiful that new day could be – I gave myself permission to expect something better and even joyful.

My visualizations became my reality. I had time for breaks. I had energy at the end of the day. My shifts ended on time. I began to notice that colleagues behaved differently toward me. They stopped to help me, even when I had not asked for their assistance. Kindness became the new normal. I was assigned easier patients and my work schedule supported me, rather than working against me.

The nurse team environment changed. I took 100 percent responsibility for my role on the team and focused on being supportive and positive.

I began to develop new and positive habits at work – to turn my once despised work environment into a playground.

I am a living proof that we can always have a better life, wherever we are at, in our lives. I transformed my life at work within few months. I feel I am dynamic after a day of work, having the effect of changing also my life outside work, I feel in better control and I quit my addiction to cigarettes.

I tell myself I deserve the best, I put the gratitude ahead, and I attract surprising situations and understand that's a free way to be able to enjoy the life at every moment. I can tell that a lot of my frustrations disappeared, I am able to appreciate were I am at, and all around me - especially at work – showed me that I am valued.

I feel part of the team. I enjoy doing what I consider now as an activity more than a work, because it occurs on what I perceive to now be like a playground: nursing.

Changing the perception is the key of manifestation modification. *When you change the way you look at things, the things you look at change.* ~Wayne Dyer, brainyquotes.com

---

Brigitte Carignan's life turned around on a difficult day in Quebec, Canada. Having begun the path to attracting a happier and more abundant life, she received a profound sign from the universe, which propelled her toward embracing a new adventure, becoming a co-author with Joe Vitale. A dedicated nurse, Brigitte is also an aspiring author living her dream life and enjoying the journey.

wealllovetoconnect.wordpress.com

One Positive Comment
Joshua Crabb

For most of us, positive thoughts come and go. Often, they're overruled by negative thoughts. One "what a beautiful day" is eclipsed by a driver flipping you off, a notification of an overdue bill, and the fear that you're going to be late for work. That single positive thought that started the day is quickly erased by a day of fear, negativity, and stress. Life continues like this unless you make it stop. The truth is that quitting negativity isn't difficult. And one positive comment is all that it really takes.

One short year ago, I was going down a path that was very self-destructive. I'd had a series of events that I believed to be bad luck.

One thing after another happened at work. I was letting it consume me. The negativity was overwhelming. I was no longer productive with my job, and my health was deteriorating quickly. I'd gained about 20 pounds and felt like a slug.

I'd sit at my desk and remind myself to breathe.

It sounds crazy, but I was forgetting to breathe. It hurt. I started seeing spots in my left eye and had developed chronic and almost unbearable headaches.

I was afraid to go to a doctor, because I knew that he'd tell me I was on the verge of having a heart attack or a stroke.

The Epiphany – The First Powerful Positive Comment of the Day

One morning, when I was getting ready for another day at work I heard my four-year-old playing in his room. Something about the way he was playing made me stop and pay attention. Peeking into his room I walked into the light. You know how children radiate light and positivity. Standing in his doorway, I watched this joyful child play. I listened as he told a story to his toys.

I realized that I was smiling. Not just smiling but grinning from ear to ear. My heart and body were filled with joy. It was a feeling that I hadn't had in a while. As I stood there watching him, I realized that I would never have that exact day and time back. It was a precious gift. Each moment of our lives is a precious gift. Right now is a gift.

You cannot respect the gift if you live your life in fear and negativity. I made a conscious decision at that point to be positive. I took my son to school that day. We played, laughed, and sang the entire way. Unlike those fleeting positive thoughts in the past, I held onto this positivity like my life depended on it – and in truth, it probably did.

I headed to work still smiling. I started saying things aloud like "it's all going to be just fine."

I can only control what I can control. I can only control myself.

I started questioning my life and my purpose. What was my legacy going to be? Surely when all is said and done my tombstone wasn't going to read, "Here lies Joshua Crabb. He lost that one big sales deal back in 2013."

I took a chance on me, knowing I had to make a positive investment in me somehow. I connected with Nahara to take an energy approach to re-center myself, solidify my steps to be positive and embody that spirit moving forward for myself and everyone I connect with.

I realized that if one positive comment had the power to change my entire perspective on life, just think what it could do for others. I created Positive Comment of the Day on Facebook. Each day I'd share a positive comment, handwritten, because writing has power to connect with your soul on a different level. I invited people to send me their positive comments, written down on paper, and I'd post them on the page. A movement began.

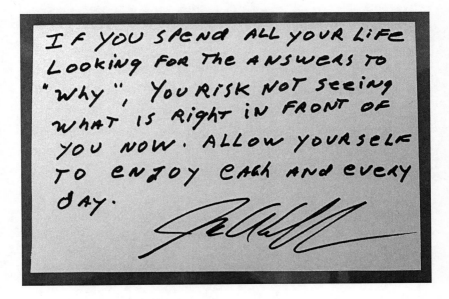

If you spend all your life looking for the answers to "why", you risk not seeing what is right in front of you now. Allow yourself to enjoy each and every day.

Why One Positive Comment Works

We get lost going day to day.

When you stop to look at the big picture, does it matter if you focus on the negative instead of the positive?

Yes. It's easier to stay focused on the negative. It takes work to clear your mind of those thoughts and fears. I know that like attracts like, and that one negative comment can quickly multiply. One positive comment has the same results – it grows stronger when you focus on it. The challenge is to decide where you're going to put your focus.

A Powerful Reminder

One Positive Comment works much like a gratitude journal. When you write down what you're grateful for, it reminds you to focus on the good in your life. The same is true for positive thoughts and comments. When you write them down, you have a powerful reminder. Simply by writing a positive thought or comment, you're committing to being positive every single day.

A Community of Support

Like attracts like, right? Now imagine how much more powerful that attraction is when you surround yourself with others who are on the same path and have the same purpose. Not only are you committing to focusing on, and attracting, positive forces and events in your life, you're also creating a movement. There's strength in that. One small voice singing is beautiful; thousands singing together is life-altering and shakes the heavens.

Awareness

By engaging in One Positive Comment, or creating your own practice, you remind yourself to become aware of your thoughts. Negative thoughts will still enter your mind. We're human and some days are difficult. Writing your positive comment for the day and keeping it with you or sharing it helps you become more aware of your thoughts, and thus gives you the power to choose. If you're unconscious about your thoughts, you can't choose them. They bubble up and control your emotions and reactions. When you're aware of them, you can take positive action and shift your energy.

Change is Waiting for You

Start writing down one thought each day. It doesn't have to be poetic or perfect. Let your soul speak and write it down. Meditate on it if you choose. Read it aloud. Fold it up and keep it with you, tuck it in a box, pin it to a board or share it with me. Do what feels right and embrace positivity. Start your snowball effect to create a positive change in your life today.

Joshua Crabb is the founder of Positive Comment of the Day. His project has given the opportunity to share the practice of Positive Thinking through, writings, speaking, Inspirational Story Telling and coaching to all, each and every day. Learn more and join the movement at www.positivecomment.net.

My Journey in the Search for Happiness

Jasmyne DesBiens

I don't remember exactly when it all started but I've been fascinated with happiness for years. I wondered: was it in a man, new friends, food, or maybe money? Whatever it was, I wanted to find it.

What was going to give me the answers? Was it esoteric, religion, the supernatural, positive thinking? What I didn't know is that there was nothing to find. It was there all along. See for yourself. Here is my journey in search of happiness.

In my younger years, I thought it must have something to do with a man. At 15, I had a serious boyfriend, and by 19 I was engaged and on my way to having kids. But by 22, I did the unthinkable. I broke off the engagement. If this was happiness, then I didn't want any part of it. I was miserable; happiness had to be something else.

I then thought it must be a career. I got a great job and worked my way up the corporate ladder. By the time I was 30, I had the title, paid vacations, and a great salary. At 31, yet again, I was miserable and did the unthinkable. Although I didn't have another job lined up, I quit. I just had to get out of there. If this was happiness, I didn't want any part of this either. I just couldn't believe I was on this earth to be miserable.

At that point, I had all the skills to start my own business. However, by now I'm sure you already figured out the pattern I was creating. Yes, again, I realized I was miserable. What was the predominant factor that guided me during all my adventures? It was ME. Yes, I was at the heart of my unhappiness.

And so began a beautiful journey that brought me here. What was that elusive concept "happiness" that I kept striving for, yet always fell short of reaching? I dug deep into what made me, me.

I always loved to study and human behavior fascinated me. I found ways to study everything and anything that interested me, even though some subjects elicited looks of disbelief or even pity.

One of the greatest lessons in my life stemmed from becoming a simultaneous translator for NLP seminars. As the French-speaking leader was lecturing, I was translating to the English participants. During this time I learned that we speak and listen at the same time. If you try this for yourself you will see that something fascinating happens: you hear the words, memorize them, and say them out loud. As you say them aloud, you listen to confirm they are the "right words." As you do this, you can't hear anymore.

This was an exceptional experience about being in the present moment. When you are speaking with someone, you are not (in your mind) finishing a job, paying your bills or figuring out the next thing you need to do. The translating team called it getting out of the way. I brought this concept into my day to day life. Today, it has transformed my relationships and, when I speak to clients, I can identify when they have voices in their heads.

A significant phrase that instigated the work I do now is: The words that come out of your mouth give you your very next moment of being alive. Therefore, I started looking at my words. I had good words. But why was I not happy? Then I started to look at, where my words came from? My mind? My thoughts. Thoughts were also at the heart of my being.

One of the major influences of my work has been Michael Neill and the Three Principles: Mind – Thought – Consciousness. Michael says, imagine your mind is a cup, your consciousness is water and your thought is a tea bag. When you drop the tea in water, the water gets flavored with what's in the bag. That's what our thoughts do to us, they add a flavor.

After all the studying I have done, I can tell you that what I know for sure is that when my mind is clear, my communication is clear and when my communication is clear, I am happy. Men, money, friends or glamour has nothing to do with it. While this is not necessarily THE truth, it is MY truth.

If you think about it, what is truth? Is the sky blue? Is water clear? The answer is not complicated. Complication is made of thought. Complication is the cloud preventing you from seeing your truth.

Remember the first time you flew through a cloud? You got to the other side, right? Thought is the same thing. Don't give it life; don't make it real. It is not solid matter. It is like a cloud.

In the quest for happiness, and the exploration of what it entailed, I found what lay at the core. I believe, in the beginning, we were all love, pure and uncluttered by thought. Then, life happened, we got hurt and we all created different ways to cope. But the love is still there, we just can't always see it. It's clutter. Fear clutter, pain clutter, past clutter. I suspect that clarity will have a strong impact on your happiness.

Be present. Catch yourself having conversations in your head. Observe all the conversations happening and identify what generated them. Notice how long you can stay there. Notice the thoughts created by thoughts. It all started with a simple thought that generated a slew of other thoughts.

Be courageous, look at what's keeping you from the life you want and clean up the thought clutter. Once clarity sets in, you will be able to create something new. If you feel that you can't do it alone, I would be honored to guide you on this all-important journey. I know that you too can be peaceful, you too can be happy.

Jasmyne is a business woman, life coach and author who dedicated the past 20 years studying communication and betterment. She has coached and trained businesses in customer relationship management and has inspired individuals to reach new levels of success by uncovering the barriers that prevent them from connecting to their wisdom. For more information, visit www.TheInspiress.com.

The Inherent Power Within

Mellisa Dormoy

Children are born without limits. They don't know the concept of the word "can't." Limitations and false beliefs are learned and carried along into adulthood. Imagine the power a child could have if they were able to grow up without these limitations and programming.

Teaching children self-esteem, self-love and personal development, allows us to transform childhood. And the truth is that we can teach children how they themselves create their own lives with their thoughts. We can educate them on how to trust and live by their inner guidance.

I'm blessed to be able to play a role in this process. As a kid, I had pretty low self-esteem. As I got older and altered my own self-image, I became fascinated with the subconscious mind and its ability to create and improve our lives. After earning a degree in Psychology, I became a clinical hypnotherapist, specializing in pediatric hypnosis.

In my work, I realized that children have an inherent power. It simply needs to be recognized and cultivated. I work with clients all over the world, and coach parents to teach children the power of their mind and our ability to create and revolutionize our life experiences through guided imagery.

One particular story of healing and success that forever stands out in my mind is that of a mother and child in Asia.

A seven-year-old boy needed an operation for an ongoing illness. He felt he had undergone too many procedures, and was always poked and prodded by doctors. The mother had continually promised to be by his side to help and protect him.

One day, while he lay on the examining table, it was determined he needed an immediate procedure to save his life. He was distraught. His pleading eyes looked to his mother for help.

This time, instead of speaking, she simply held his body down as the panicked seven-year-old began to scream and wail. His bewildered eyes expressed disbelief at her broken promise to protect him. She was trying to help him, but in his mind it was him against the world. The following day, he stopped speaking to her. He stopped hugging her. He stopped giving her kisses goodnight.

The mother had ordered a set of CDs from me to help her child, who had refused to acknowledge her in any way for over two years. In a three-page email to me, she expressed the most profound gratitude.

After listening to one of my audio meditations speaking of love, her son awoke, walked to her and with the first morning kiss in over two years... said "I'm so sorry Mommy. I was so angry at you. I thought you were hurting me when you held me down. I thought you didn't love me anymore." This was the beginning of the healing of the relationship between this beautiful child and his heartbroken mother.

I cried as I read her email. Healing sometimes requires a catalyst, and I felt (and continue to feel) so very blessed and grateful to have been able to be a part of that. This is true success. Sharing the core of who we are with others, in whichever way we choose to manifest that sharing – this is success at its finest.

Deep inside we all desire to experience deep love and connection.

When we help another feel and access that unconditional love within themselves – through example, motivational words, inspiration or guided imagery like in my work – we are ALL enriched. I am incredibly blessed to do what I do because I absolutely love the joy I create in my unique service to humanity.

I feel like we are each given a precious gift with each breath we take. To make ourselves small or insignificant is just atrocious. We are born creators and leaders with unique and wondrous gifts to share – each and every one of us! Our core, being pure unadulterated love, can express itself in mind-blowing uniquely ways. There is no other more powerful strategy than allowing our hearts to continually guide us, and then simply stepping up to fulfill our unique mission with all our heart's passion.

The greatest asset to my success, and one that I believe we can and should teach children, has been knowing that life is really one big beautiful spiritual journey. Its opportunities for growth and its soul challenges allow me to remain humble and content even in the face of adversity. I sense everything flows together for the highest good, even when I cannot control the outcome. I have faith and I remember to laugh at myself and at the humor and irony life mirrors to us.

Mellisa Dormoy is a children's guided imagery trainer dedicated to helping children realize their inherent power within. Her business, ShambalaKids, is aimed at teaching guided imagery for self-improvement through programs, CDs and classes. Mellisa is currently training professionals in children's guided imagery and relaxation classes for kids. www.shambalakids.com

Affirmations Don't Work For Everybody

Constantine Dovlatov

W hy do I say this?

My name is Constantine Dovlatov. I live in Moscow, Russia. I have two university degrees – one in physics and the other in psychology. I have a degree in psychology, and I run my own coaching school and school of applied psychology where I teach techniques of spiritual development. I am a millionaire, which is quite uncommon among psychologists.

I have more than ten thousand customers and more than a thousand students, and I accumulated quite lot data through observation as result of my job. My experience in observation of customers and students is quite rich.

I was born in a poor family and grew up without a father. My mother was forced to beg. We had very little. Moreover I was very weak and sickly child. However, I always wondered how could I change my life and become successful in everything I did.

I came across books about positive thinking, affirmations and so on, but unfortunately they did not work for me. I could convince myself of anything for months. I even learned autogenic training and during several months twice a day tried to "become more confident day after day." But ultimately nothing worked.

So I started to practice autogenic journey. I was traveling in internal space, which opened up to me in the state between sleeping and waking. In one of these trips I wandered in a cemetery with many tombstones. And each of the formulas of self-hypnosis that I've ever applied was engraved on a tombstone. The cemetery was filled with my failed suggestions and affirmations. At that moment I realized that my subconscious does not accept any self-hypnosis.

Autogenic journey, unlike the suggestions, began to yield results. In these journeys I recalled the most difficult and painful moments of my childhood and relived them again in new ways, with different behaviors. And that brought results.

Much later, after I became an experienced psychologist with thousands of hours of practice, I examined my failures and identified 13 types of obstacles to a prosperous life. Everybody faces these obstacles to some extent or other. I used this knowledge when working with my students and clients. The results catch the imagination. Sometimes just 30-40 minutes is enough to transform a person into someone who can achieve success in a few months, or even days.

What are these 13 magic obstacles on your way to prosperous life?

I'll share the first three with examples from my life and the lives of my clients.

1. Traumas

The most important obstacles are traumas, and really we're talking about psychological traumas here. These are situations where you experience unpleasant emotions, which last for some time – even after the situation is over.

One of my students, poor as a church mouse, recalled his trauma. His father gave him money and asked him to buy something at the market. The boy lost the money and could not buy anything. He came home and told his father about it. The father gave him a whipping. It was painful; he felt bitterness and his feelings were hurt. But it was much more painful later. Every time when his father gave him money, he reminded and humiliated his son over the previous loss, saying that he had "holes in his pockets."

This guy is already 50 years old and he is still losing money. This son follows the way of his father – he humiliates himself every time when dealing with money. This trauma influenced almost everything in his life – his finance, the level of self-esteem (very low) and relationships with people in general (and women in particular). At age 50 he was still single with no prospect of marriage. The cleaning of this trauma and related problems took almost 10 hours. Now he is 52, and married with a child on the way.

2. Secondary Gains

Secondary gains are a magic way to make trauma an ally. For example if you are sick you can get insurance payment. You don't have to work or pick up children from school, and you can read or watch TV as long as want.

If not for being sick you might feel like you're in paradise. Do you think your illness will pass quickly? Most likely not. After all it has so many secondary gains!

One friend of mine, a stock market trader, did everything to lose all her money through self-sabotage. She bought shares of companies that were one step from bankruptcy, even as she managed her customers' accounts more prudently. As a consequence she lost her own money. Even though she did a good job for her customers, SHE HAS PERFECT EXCUSE TO COMPLAIN ABOUT HER LIFE! We have removed this and many other secondary gains in 2 hours. We did it recently, but there are already positive dynamics in her personal investments.

3. Associations

This is biochemical bond between pleasant and unpleasant emotions. As a result, one is always accompanied by another one. If it's love and fear, then a person chooses a partner he is afraid of. If it is safety and sadness, he will always be sad. Should he start to enjoy, he begins to feel danger. Associations originate during pre-natal period and childhood. We have hundreds of them. Welfare is influenced by associations of wealth and fear, opportunities and confusion, love and poverty.

In the Russian culture if a child hurts themselves, adults around say: "My poor, my unlucky." Thanks to this common saying, most of people have an association of love, poverty and misery. And every time we want to be loved, we do everything to fail and become miserable. And the subconscious mind decides that we are not poor or unlucky enough, and works to make us ever increasingly poor and unlucky, for years and decades...

Discover the other 10 magic obstacles that may be impeding your success and happiness. Visit http://dowlatow.ru/books/midastouch to download a recording made just for you - increase your physical and emotional health.

Trust Your Heart

Geeta Dubey

I t's not always easy to be in the moment and to have faith that it's all going to work out. Dreams can be so big that the fear of not achieving them may overwhelm. Not so good things happen in life to put doubt into your heart and mind. The only way to regain a sense of calm and trust is to let go and believe in what you hear and feel from your heart.

I was born in India and always had a dream to go to the United States of America. I grew up in a typical middle-class Indian family. We're raised to believe that we have to study hard and that they're a proper path to follow. You get your degree in a respectable field, you work, you get married and you have a family.

I followed the rules. I didn't mind. I was inclined to study as all the other students were and I was going to study to become a pharmacist/doctor. Yet, I was also very passionate about colors and gemstones and always have been fascinated by them. I received my bachelor's degree in India and I became a pharmacist there. The passion for gemstones and for going to America never faded. When I expressed the desire to go to America to my mother, she told me that I could get married or have a job there.

So I got married to a very wonderful person and we moved to

the United States. He was working on his Master's degree in Engineering at that time and I joined a pharmaceutical company where I worked as a scientist. I enjoyed what I was doing – it was actually interesting, analytical, and focused work.

We started a family and after I had my second son I took a break from work. I started doing something at home just collecting gemstones and beading. My family encouraged me to start selling my jewelry. Then while I was online, I saw an ad on Craigslist advertising a retail location. It was a great location and led me to open my first boutique.

A young girl with dreams of going to America and a passion for jewelry. I held onto those dreams, but not so tightly that the Universe couldn't respond. I allowed life to lead me and I trusted the process. Now I'm an adult living in America with a jewelry boutique. I imagined it and it happened better than I could ever have believed.

Of course it's never as easy as it looks. There were moments where I doubted my path and purpose in life. Many of those difficult moments are fleeting. You take a deep breath, regroup, and forge ahead. Other moments are more difficult.

The darkest time in my life was when my son became sick and ended up in the hospital for several weeks. I felt helpless. I questioned everything. Why was he there? What did I do wrong? There had to be a reason, everything happens for a reason, right? So why was my son suffering? What was the lesson? Where was the silver lining? This was the lowest part of my life. I almost closed my business and staying away from everybody and just taking care of my son as my motherly instincts took over. I felt like I needed to protect your child from everything.

I realized that I had to be the strength for everyone. I couldn't fall apart, I needed to be the role model. I started working on myself for a change. We were all on the journey together and it was difficult for everyone.

"Open heart and an open mind". Then I became a real student of life and learned valuable lessons of life from mentors like my parents, brother, sister, husband - Rajeev, my two sons - Dhruv and Dhwaj, Michel Suissa, friends and all my clients.

My studies and reflection taught or reminded me of a few things. The first is that gratitude is essential. You have to have a very open heart about everything. There's always something to be grateful for. I began to do a morning gratitude practice. I would say to the family when they called, everything is good, everything is fine a very positive outlook.

And I used to do five minutes of breathing exercises which led me to become a certified Meditation Instructor. I'd do it with my children. It was something that we could all do together to become more aware, relaxed and hopeful as well as to connect with each other. I practiced yoga, we began to drink more water, and just take better care of ourselves. I led the charge, but you have to be responsible for yourself too.

After doing working on myself, I began thinking anything is possible, you can really do it, if you put your mind, your heart, your body or your soul to it actually. And those exercises helped my business, my entrepreneurial spirit too.

I was a very numbers oriented person in my business. That's fine. However, I started to realize that if you just add a little bit of spirituality or something more mindful you'll be much happier at the end of the day. I was able to shift my focus and now as soon as a person comes in to my boutique, I see them as a client but also as a person. I serve, I have compassion, and there's a connection. They're more than a potential profit in my eyes.

Of course, I am there as an entrepreneur to sell things, but that really started giving me peace and now when I talk with them, I share experiences , they laugh and it just puts a smile on their faces and it makes a huge difference. For me now smile is **See My**self **In Love Everyday.**

That was my turning point.

Before, I felt like I didn't have a clue. The exercises, practices, and trust make differences to you as a person and as an entrepreneur, you can do them and you find gratification toward what you are heading for and you feel it actually. As a pharmacist I was seeing and learning about the heart, now I am hearing it and feeling it too.

Born and brought up in India, I was convinced by my surroundings to pursue a scientific career which means I was a pharmacist before I was able to discover myself. There was this latent desire about the artistic side of the world that I always attracted me but stayed away from me until about 10 years back. Eventually, the inner voice led me to open up my jewelry and clothing boutique without any formal training. The rediscovered journey had barely begun when a low phase in my personal life forced me to rediscover myself - again! The result was my growing belief in spirituality and finding

simplicity in an otherwise chaotic thought process. It taught me to trust my heart and elevated & purify my analytical thoughts to a meditative state, eventually leading to my certification in meditation as well. All those experiences taught me the valuable lesson to always trust my heart and more importantly believe in the universe! I urge everyone to at least take one moment in the day to SMILE (See Myself In Love Everyday). This is my journey - from a heartless diva to a heartful diva. Learn more about me at www.geetasboutique.com.

3 BS Excuses Made By Entrepreneurs Who Resist Success

Eric Du Pont

What have you done to attract and achieve what you want in life? Many people say that they want this or that. For example, they want more success or more wealth, but at the end of the day, they really don't want it.

You can kick and scream and insist that you really do want something different. The truth is that you've created exactly what you have. The outcome of your life is precisely the one you asked for.

Day after day I come across people (family, friends, colleagues, or clients I coach) who tell me they want to start a business or grow their business. What I hear from them is funny. I call them the BS excuses. And to be honest, I've personally experienced all of them at some point in my life and I appreciate every single one of them, for the clarity each gave me and my NOW ability to smell the bull before I end up in the pile.

BS Excuse #1
"I Need To Focus On Saving Money Right Now. Money Is Tight."

That's a fancy way of saying that you don't believe in yourself and in your ability to create the results you say you want, not to mention the toll on your health, your relationships and your joy. There, we just touched on it: your JOY!!! (And you thought we were talking about money!)

How are you doing in the "joy" department while worrying about money and living less than you intended, all in the name of fixing your finances?

You know you're tight on money, now. You're repeating that line to everyone who will listen. Newsflash: do you think you're focusing on making it better by talking about the lack of money, and trying to fix it by spending less, saving more, working harder …?

How's that working out for you?

The thing is, as much as you are fixating on the problem you're facing, you can't get to the real solution! You won't find the solution while fixated on the problem.

You know something about people with money? They never talk about money. Money is just a resource we use, like the air we all breathe. Are you worried about your next breath? Of course not. You know it will be there, as sure as you KNOW the sun is going to rise in the morning.

What are you EXPECTING in your life? Wherever you are in your life, START now, designing your life and transforming your business from the inside out.

Excuse #2
"I'm Already in Debt, I Can't Afford to Invest in Myself."

Yeah, so what?

Billionaire entrepreneur Richard Branson was reportedly over $400 million in debt, before his business became profitable.

Entrepreneurs who KNOW that their success is inevitable may not like going further in debt as they wait for their breakthrough, and it might be stressful, but they have the tenacity to keep going because they SEE THEIR FUTURE and refuse to quit on themselves.

Prioritizing debt issues before creating your dreams is akin to saying you believe there is limited abundance and limited money available, so therefore you can't afford to "risk" more of your finances.

What if, instead, you created the atmosphere that is conducive to that which you want, and in so doing, the very things that you want come to you?

That's right: I'm talking ATTRACTION here.

What if you took inspired action to the steps that you know will yield you the results you want? Do YOURSELF a favor, stop using the BS excuse of debt, which is nothing more than the results of your previous beliefs, and get started NOW, designing your life and transforming your business from the inside out, one thought and one action at a time.

Excuse #3 "I Don't Really Know What I Want, Yet."

It cracks me up to watch people look at a menu, unable to decide what they want, taking 20 minutes to pick their meal, finally making a decision after asking twenty questions about each of the items, and still agonizing as to whether they made the right choice.

Enough, already... It's just one meal. Pick something and decide to enjoy it. Find what's tasty about it; revel in the texture and the sight of your delicious dish.

Trust your gut instinct.

Trust that what you picked was right for you, because it is. Give yourself permission and choose to get started NOW. Design your life and transform your business from the inside out, one thought at a time.

Take the first step and I promise you, the next step will reveal itself to you, as will the next, and the next.

Today Is A New Day

As Nina Simone's song, "Feeling Good," goes, "it is a new dawn, it's a new day, it's a new life" ... and a new opportunity to choose. As a matter of fact, everyday you wake up is a fresh start; a rebirth of sorts. Your slate was wiped clean while you slept.

Wouldn't it be nice if you started your day with different thoughts from the sucky ones you went to bed with? YOU can create the atmosphere in your mind, the feeling in your heart of appreciation, of clarity, of freedom and security.

Wouldn't it be nice if your experience was one of ease and peace in your thoughts, of contentment with where you are, and eagerness for what is coming, reveling in the knowing that you are having fun on the way to the dreams and the big vision you have for your life?

What a wonderful journey we are in. Why not live more, enjoy more, bask more, allow more? There is no risk; there only is the continuation of life and the realization of joy here and now. Wake up. Quit the BS excuses. Let go of limiting beliefs, thoughts, and actions. Start DESIGNING your life, your business, your lifestyle from the inside out.

Eric Du Pont is an Intuitive Coach, Entrepreneur, Business Consultant and Pilot who is designing and transforming his own life and supporting people in re-discovering the tools that will empower them to do the same, with intention. Book your FREE 30-minute Clarity Session with him at www.ericjoeldupont.com.

It Changed My Entire Outlook on Life!

Helena Ederveen

How many of us have been conditioned and manipulated to believe that we cannot have what we desire. We are been told over and over again to get real and get down to earth!

Be normal, and so on. However, what it means to be normal was never being explained other than that I have to comply with what the norm is within society.

I was confronted with a lot of limiting beliefs and was told over and over again that I was not normal. That I needed to get with my feet on the ground and do what society would accept.

There was a lot of hypocrisy in my "education." At a young age I started to question a lot of issues and the response was always that I needed to get my feet on the ground. You will discover this in the time to come!! Indeed I did. I became pregnant when I was 16 years old and was petrified.

Then the name of the family had to be rescued, and hence there were two choices. The first one was that I needed to have an abortion. This was unacceptable to me since during my years prior to the pregnancy I was being told that this was murder. Suddenly this value was rejected, and since I refused to travel to Switzerland the marriage had to be arranged.

Life always presents us with opportunities for transformation and surely this was one of them.

In hindsight it has been a very valuable lesson to discover what true love means, and what a marriage out of obligation is.

Between the age of 6 and 16, I was placed in a convent and discovered a lot of hypocrisy. Over time I started to question and investigate the value of the different religions.

The nuns were very rigid, and some of them were very cruel and used nasty devices to punish us. One example was that we were not allowed to go to the toilet during the night, and after I was caught out, the next night I was woken up and told I had to go to the shower and bathroom to be taught a lesson. One of the nuns sprayed me with ice cold water for quite some time, and in hindsight I realized she enjoyed doing this.

It is important to mention that I was sent to the convent when I was 6 years old and became isolated from my family in many ways.

One day, when I discovered that my older sister was no longer in the convent and I questioned my mother about this, she said you are strong enough and this was the end of the conversation.

At a young age I made a decision that I didn't wanted to be involved with the Catholic Church anymore. And this was not to the liking of my mother. She was brought up in a very strict Protestant environment, however when she met my father she decided to become a Catholic. And she became fanatic.

One day, when I told my mum that I was going to investigate the different religions, she told "when you do that I will make sure you are not in my last will anymore." I couldn't have cared less.

When a priest came to my parents' house, they asked him for advice about my attitude. The priest told my parents that it didn't matter which religion was appealing to me, as long as it connected me with my spiritual values. Wow that was music to my ears!

At the age of 72, I feel so blessed for all the amazing experiences I have had in my life.

One of the most important lessons I learned was how to take my own power back and listen to my intuition.

I also realized that being born in a highly dysfunctional family has taught me many lessons, and hence I developed a deep empathy for people and their challenges. And helping people to hold themselves up to the mirror, and teach them how to take their own power back, is one of the most rewarding things in my life.

Once the willingness it there, it is amazing how we can develop a deep love and empathy for ourselves, and hence for other people too. And this willingness and readiness will have a major impact on the physical, mental and spiritual health. This is how it was meant to be!

You can choose to learn how to create your life that makes you sing and begin to understand that no one else but you create your life experiences. You can choose to live a life based upon Domination or on Dominion.

You can choose to live a life based in good emotional and physical health. One of the important things to realize is that every physical condition has an underlying emotional connection. Without the integration of the emotional connection you will keep on chasing your own tail and never find lasting solutions.

Did you know that while we are in the womb we "adopt" certain emotional genetic patterns that have been passed on from generation to generation? Some of these emotions passed along to you can be positive. However, when they are not positive and limiting they can be easily removed and replaced with more supportive patterns.

As a clinical nutritionist and certified master practitioner in neuro-linguistic programming and Ericksonian hypnosis, I practice what I preach and have been blessed to be a guide for health education with self-growth. I've been able to not only clear my own programming, but have also helped many people live a life they choose. Today is the day to start clearing, and to choose a better life.

Helena Ederveen is a Holistic Healthcare Practitioner and nutritionist with certifications in NLP and Advanced Eriksonian Hypnosis. Helena specializes in treating people with sleep apnea, fibromyalgia, fatigue, depression, and other health challenges. If you're struggling with health problems, visit www.HelenaEderveen.com and sign up for a free consultation.

Critical Moments
Craig Fuller

In every moment you have a choice.
You can see the limitation before you,
or you can see the abundance before you.

~ Joe Vitale, THE ABUNDANCE MANIFESTO

During my three decades in Washington, D.C., the *critical moments* that leaders confront, and the manner in which they work through the complex issues associated with these moments, often define individuals for years or even a lifetime. Given the importance of successfully managing through a critical moment, you might think people carefully prepare in advance for these defining events. They don't.

The question is: do you?

As a pilot for more than 45 years who has flown everything from a light two-seater aircraft to a business jet, the skills my fellow aviators and I learn and practice offer what I have always found to be important lessons in life.

Preparation is essential when you fly airplanes. The lessons learned from studying *critical moments* in aviation accidents have informed pilot training since the Wright brothers. Now, with the availability of flight simulators for all types of aircraft, we can pre-pare for emergencies and experience situations that most of us will never actually see during a lifetime of flying.

A pilot seeing the onset of a possible engine failure will begin climbing. Altitude gives the pilot more options if there is an engine failure.

For some malfunctions there are memory items that are drilled into pilots. When flying at high altitude and seeing any indication of pressurization issues, for instance, don the oxygen mask immediately. Maybe there is just a faulty reading on an instrument, but no pilot suffering from hypoxia can successfully troubleshoot in flight issues.

There are many examples, but all lead to the same point; well trained and experienced pilots, facing a *critical moment*, will always take actions that give them better options. Said another way, they will seek *abundance* and avoid *limitations*.

Whether you pilot an aircraft, or manage a business or a house-hold, favoring abundance and avoiding limitations will determine how successfully you work through your own critical moments.

Consider these aviation related perspectives…

1. *Gain Altitude*

It is obvious that an aircraft further from the ground when trouble hits will have more options. The same is true if you build a strong positive reputation and have many loyal friends.

During my early White House years, a wise colleague said that a President is either making deposits into his political bank account or taking something out. Knowing that there would be times when political capital would need to be spent, we worked very hard to build political capital every day.

Build your own personal capital through strong relationships and a favorable reputation.

2. *Train*

An engine failure in my twin engine Baron shortly after takeoff presents a critical moment. The reaction is the same: throttle, propeller and fuel controls forward; fuel pumps on; determine which engine has failed; throttle back and feather the propeller of the failed engine; lower the nose to reach single engine climb speed to continue the climb; and declare an emergency. There is no time for uncertainty and no time to consult a manual. I have done this dozens of times… in a simulator, but never once in actual flight. However, knowing what to do and thinking about it every time I take off gives me an abundance of options should I face a critical moment in the form of an in flight emergency.

Life back on the ground certainly can bring many challenges. However, you can train for the unexpected. First, expect the unexpected. Like the pilot above, keep flying the plane. Work through a mental checklist. Understand what must be done to provide more options and not limit them. Learn what is actually happening and address it. Reduce the possibility that one issue will drag you or your enterprise down. Honestly state the nature of the problem to those who can help.

3. Fit to fly

Even the most experienced pilots ask themselves "am I fit to fly?" before every flight. This assessment saves lives and it is something that those of us who fly aircraft take so seriously it guides the way we lead our lives. Alcohol, drugs, obesity and stress can all limit our ability to do something we love to do – fly airplanes. The "fit to fly" question also pertains to the aircraft and here, too, the experienced pilot carefully checks all the factors related to a safe flight before leaving the ground.

When I hear someone suggest they "…really need a clear head today," I wonder what they think they need the rest of the days in the week!

The very fitness factors that pilots consider before a flight are ones everyone should consider. Abuse of substances and stress probably cause more people to focus on limitations in life than anything else imaginable. And, since *critical moments* often appear with little warning, making sure you can successfully work through them really does mean being fit for flight all the time.

4. *Enjoy the trip*

I can truthfully say that for over 45 years I have enjoyed every hour I've spent in the cockpit. Sure, it is a treat to be aloft on beautiful sunny day. It is also a joy to see thunderstorms at night (as long as you're not inside one). I have enjoyed flying in snowstorms. And, I have marveled at how we can take off in poor weather, never see the ground and land hours later breaking out of solid weather to see the runway right in front of us.

The point is you never want to stop enjoying what you are doing at the moment. A positive and joyful attitude not only makes for a better experience, it provides a level of alertness and confidence to deal with the rare and unusual critical moment successfully. I have learned after thousands of hours in flight to enjoy every moment, respect the wonder of flight and have the confidence to manage the risks associated with this wondrous activity.

It is how I have led my life as well.

I hope the perspectives offered here help you successfully manage the *critical moments* in life. If you get through those, the rest really does fall into place.

Craig Fuller serves as a senior advisor to organizations and individuals drawing upon over three decades of leadership positions in Washington, D.C., which have taken him from The White House to corporations and associations. He currently works on aviation policy issues and remains an active pilot. Learn more at: www.TheFullerCompany.com

The Light Chasers
Fabrizio Galli and Fabiana Rego

"Every moment of light and dark is a miracle"

There's a small window in the back of the shop that my family has run for over 60 years. It opens east to the hills of the beautiful Italian countryside, a region where the bright sun shines over sunflower plantations during spring, and where the north wind blows, announcing the chilly, cloudy, gray days of winter season. Since I was a kid I've helped my family in the shop. I remember that window always closed, covered and blocked by useless things that nobody would dare to touch or move away. To my father, those things seemed to be the most important things in the world.

One day, someone from the shop next to mine asked me if I had noticed the weather was quickly changing at east. "Come here, look from my window," he said. "The view from this place is amazing!" I thought. Our building sits on the top of a hill. The landscape is so beautiful and unique! I came back to my shop. I removed all the stuff that was obstructing my window. I patiently cleaned the very dirty glass. Finally I got back my personal view of the landscape and a very beautiful light spread through my shop. At that precise moment, I had a grasp on life, and the reasons why black and white photography became my passion.

Until that moment, I had lived imprisoned in patterns that don't belong to me. My dreams confined in dark corners of my soul, with no light. Just like my shop. I was living by familial and social rules of a small Italian province, too small to dare looking beyond the hills. A life assumed to follow my father's step in the family business. I was taught to be rational and predictable, to put business before family, and to work hard with no time to enjoy life. I used to be extremely polite and diplomatic as an attempt to please everybody, never making my point, just looking for the neutral hues. But life is all about taking a clear position, just like black and white photography – so easy and simple if you're able to grasp the concept.

From the moment I opened that window, I knew I had to inform my father that his time at the business was over. He had to step back and let me take control over my life.

I also knew that 10,000 miles away from that window, somewhere by the Atlantic Ocean, there was a beautiful woman taking pictures of the sand and the sea. She introduced me to photography. She is my life. She is my wife.

Few weeks before, my wife Fabiana, who I deeply love, had told me that we should take some time apart. The feeling I had after trying to understand this subtle concept was like of someone who suddenly wakes up from a long sleep. The awakening was terrifying. It felt like a cold shower. It was as if up until that point I had been drugged, absent. I had been absent from myself first of all. Losing sight of myself, had I lost sight of my wife? The pain was so great that I still find it difficult to define it. What I know for sure is that not just my life had changed since then but, above all, that announcement changed me.

"We cast a shadow on something whenever we stand"

That sunny day in the tropics was an enlightened experience. My husband Fabrizio, the only person I wanted to be with on that special day, was miles away. I had to celebrate my birthday alone. I had left Italy, after living there for over a decade. That was a turning point in my life. Only the sea song of the waves could soothe the pain and the bemusement of such decision. I wanted to send him a SOS message in a bottle. "He will never get the message," I told myself. He lives in the countryside, far away from the sea, surrounded by hills, effectively held hostage by them.

I grew up by the sea, enchanted by the salt smell and the idea of freedom. That nickel-silver line that is the horizon in the tropics was an invitation to ventures beyond the sea. I left my family, friends and a promising career. I had a good time, learned new skills, visited different countries and cultures. I met my husband, who I love profoundly. I settled down.

At some point, I started to look back, questioning how I had turned into a "perfect" – and unhappy – Italian (house)wife. The enthusiasm had gone away, alongside with the capacity to focus and persevere to reach my own goals. I used to walk down the streets looking up to the sky, amused by the beauty of things. I realized I've spent too long looking down and staring the shadows instead. Was I losing the ability to dream and to fight for things that I truly wish? That thought scared me to death. I headed to the nearest post office and finally sent my husband a message in a bottle: "I'm looking for THE KEY to rediscover THE MAGIC of life and restart with ZERO LIMITS. These books are your late birthday presents. You reading them is your present to me."

The light at the end of the tunnel

We both started reading those books daily. Page after page, it became a sort of countdown until we could meet again. Days became weeks. Weeks became months. Words written in those pages were impressed in our minds, then in our hearts. The stories of people who overcame traumas, difficulties and losses of all sorts, as well as of those who failed and then succeeded, against all odds, in every aspect of their lives, were of great inspiration. We are deeply glad for such words of wisdom.

As we progressed on a deep journey within ourselves, we started feeling again that kind of soul and mind connection we had lost. Like someone who could watch but not see, Fabrizio started to rediscover life through the lens of his photography camera. The chase of the perfect light became the chase of the meaning of life itself. Every picture taken is a way to capture an emotion. Fabiana continued her ever growing wish to frame the true beauty of people in form of pictures and putting into words her travel experiences. Yet, we were still to discover the light at the end of the tunnel.

Would we still be able to rebuild our marriage? Would we be courageous to admit we were not living our lives to the fullest? When you awaken at all, knowing intimately to live in a deep misery, you have to take a clear position. And a leap of faith.

The Lighthouse

The phone rang. "That marriage of us as has come to an end. We've tried many things. We've changed. Do you remember the one thing we never, ever stopped thinking about?" asked Fabrizio. "So, when do we meet there?" Fabiana replied.

Another month passed and it seemed the longest of our lives. The clock ticked 3pm when the train stopped at final destination. A small town boy walked towards the city girl.

We looked into each other eyes. We had really changed, almost to the point of not recognizing each other. There was a new light in our eyes. That old life of us was over. But all ends with new beginnings. The old version of us was replaced by stronger individuals. In a bright sunny day in one of the most grayish of the cities, we felt we belonged to each other. Back to London, we felt at home.

It's not easy to explain what happened from that moment on.

We had found the key to unlock the magic to pursue a fulfilling life with no limits. Overnight we made a business plan, gathering every cent we had, planning and taking risks. We were determined set up our photography business in London. We want our photos to be witnesses of other people's love stories and our own chronicles, testimonials of the city we most love. It's a dream coming true. It's a life project!

Every single day since then, we see signs from the Universe pointing us in the right direction, through coincidences that have allowed us to quickly build our portfolio, make the right connections, be featured in magazines and find new clients. It is hard work, but it is something we believe in. And when you have faith, the Universe conspires in helping you to achieve it. Chasing the perfect light to most beautiful photos, we ended up finding the lighthouse that guided us throughout the storm along our right path.

Fabrizio Galli, photographer and businessman, and Fabiana Rego, journalist and Brazillian native, are founders of londonlifeandstyle.com His black and white street photographs and her colorful, vivid articles about London has made the site a reference for those moving to the capital or just visiting.

The Social Age -
5 Laws Your Brand
Must Know to "Click" On
Social Media

Bob Hutchins

93% of marketers use social media for business.[1]

There are 1 million small and medium-sized business advertising on Facebook.[2]

Social media has a 100% higher lead-to-close rate than outbound marketing.[3]

To use or not to use social media marketing? That is... no longer the question. Businesses of all sizes, from rogue freelancers to PepsiCo, have been employing these strategies for years. The value of social media marketing isn't news.

But the "why" is still up for debate.

---

1   http://blog.hootsuite.com/5-social-media-facts-every-marketing-professor-should-know/

2   http://www.jeffbullas.com/2014/09/09/11-social-media-marketing-facts-statistics-need-know/

3   http://www.hubspot.com/marketing-statistics#Social%20Media

Why *do* we use social media? I'm not asking about the practical reasons (targeted advertising capabilities, fast and easy A/B testing, etc.). I'm interested in knowing why, as brands, we choose to communicate in this style. Searching out the answers to that question led to the development of what I call the Five Laws of the Social Age.

Five Laws of the Social Age

The Five Laws of the Social Age explain:

- How consumers communicate with one another.

- How consumers communicate with brands (and vice versa).

- Why brands that "get" the Social Age are crushing the competition.

Every marketer I know is more than capable of setting up a Facebook page for a brand. But few understand the underlying sociological and cultural patterns that turn an average-performing business page into a highly engaging, lead generating, sales-driving machine. Ready to dive in and learn what most marketers are oblivious to?

#1 Consumer Confidence

Prior to the Social Age, consumers had little recourse for determining the quality of a product. For the most part, innovation was pushed by adversarial competition (brand one-upmanship). Consumers had to trust that Brand X's product really was better than Brand Y's – just like the ad said.

Sure, you had *Consumer Reports*, chats around the water cooler, and maybe a few product demos. But ultimately, the only way to know for sure if a product did what it said was to buy it and try it yourself. That's not saying a whole lot for "consumer confidence."

Now, in the Social Age, it's an entirely different ballgame.

Between Amazon reviews, free return shipping, YouTubers, bloggers, and a slew of social media platforms, consumers can learn a lot about a product – and its competitors – before they make a purchase. In turn, this forces brands to continue innovating and revising their product or service at a faster rate than ever before. The result? Consumer confidence is at an all-time high.

#2 Authenticity

Authenticity is the cornerstone of everything that can make the Social Age a bonanza for brands and marketers. Let's face it… we're decades past the point where everyone realized an ad is an ad. In other words, *clearly* brands are showing their better side when they put up a billboard or run a TV spot.

During the Mass Media Age (early 1900s–early 2000s), slick packaging, full media control, and very little online/social conversation allowed many brands to get along just fine without so much as a dash of authenticity.

In the Social Age, that changed. On the whole, consumers don't believe that your ad is telling the truth. Now, more than ever before, brands have to be authentic. With social media, "image management" is impossible to do. If you want to *look like X*, you have to go out and *be X*.

As Rohit Bhargava writes in *Personality Not Included*, "Every company that consumers are passionate about already understands that sharing an authentic identity inspires loyalty and belief."[4] Take Apple, Nike, and Red Bull as archetypes.

So, how can you be authentic?

1. Don't project a false image. That means no stonewalling, sugar-coating, or moderate responses to questions and complaints. You'll be found out.

---

4 Rohit Bhargava, Personality Not Included: Why Companies Lose Their Authenticity and How Great Brands Get it Back, 4.

2. Show your fun side – not your good side. When you show your "good side," you're usually focused on covering up or avoiding your "bad side."

3. Fess up to screw-ups.

#3 Transparency

If authenticity is *how* you say something, then transparency is what you're actually communicating. Transparency is all about how much you communicate. Finding the sweet spot for your brand is a challenge every business has to face in the Social Age. (It's also something every individual has to decide for themselves in the Social Age – what do you share on social media? Who do you share it with?)

As marketing veteran and educator Beth Harte suggests, there are three degrees of transparency:

-   **Full Transparency:** *All the light passes through.* These companies don't run on a script when talking to consumers. Communications are up to the discretion of service reps and brand communicators.

-   **Translucency:** *Light passes through, but full images may be blocked.* Communication is somewhere between "Full Transparency" (see above) and "Opacity" (see below).

-   **Opacity:** *Some light passes through, but the image is significantly obscured.* These companies limit interactions with customers to problem solving and scripted replies.

It's up to you to decide how much "light" you allow to pass through. Just know – consumers' expectations in the Social Age are greater, and transparency is highly valued. My advice: let your human side draw people in.

#4 Responsiveness

Did you know that 42% of customers expect a response on social media in 60 minutes or less?[5] Or that the level of consumer engagement with companies on Facebook and Twitter has grown by 178% since the end of 2012?[6] Real-time response is key in the Social Age.

Brands no longer have a choice. Being "always on" and ready to respond to your consumers' needs and questions is critical. When responsiveness is consistently authentic and timely, the payoff is a snowball effect of spreading consumer recommendations that millions of dollars spent on Super Bowl commercials and other media ads will never match.

#5 Ratings and Reviews

The Social Age is dominated by ratings and reviews. The good news is that ratings and reviews are one of the easiest entry doors to social media marketing. In case you're not convinced of the power of reviews in the Social Age…

- 84% of people trust social media user reviews more than critics' reviews (Marketing Sherpa).

- 78% say consumer recommendations are the most credible form of advertising (Nielsen).

One of our main observations in the Social Age is that consumers are actively evaluating and discussing products and services. If you can harness the energy of positive reviews, you'll be able to truly capitalize on the Social Age.

---

5 http://www.convinceandconvert.com/the-social-habit/42-percent-of-con-sumers-complaining-in-social-media-expect-60-minute-response-time/

6 http://buzzplant.com/new-study-chatty-customers-social-getting-slow-response-time/

But glowing reviews aren't the only good ones to have. Negative reviews (inevitable for any business) can also help you out in the Social Age. (See the footnote for more on this topic.[7])

So... Why Do We Use Social Media?

To bring it all back around, our primary motivator for using social media isn't the bells and whistles that it adds to your brand. It isn't even the significant bump in leads and sales. Don't *get me wrong* – these benefits are great, and worth getting excited about! They're *huge* motivators! However, seeing these results requires a strategy that's firmly rooted in an understanding of the Social Age.

Facebook, Twitter, Instagram... these are all just tools. Our team at BuzzPlant has spent countless hours with these platforms: tweaking, optimizing, innovating, and pushing their capabilities to the limit.

If you don't understand the underlying sociological and cultural implications of the Social Age, as outlined in this chapter, you can't be truly effective in social media marketing. Platforms and communication styles come and go every week. But, for as far out as we can see, the Social Age is here to stay. And brands that understand it *will win*.

Want to Talk? Schedule a Free 30-Minute Consultation.

The social media marketing landscape changes overnight. New tools, best practices, and policy adjustments can significantly impact your strategy. That's a guarantee.

So, we'd like to offer you a free half-hour phone consultation with one of our social media marketing experts. There's no catch. Just send an email to info@buzzplant.com to schedule your phone consultation.

---

7   http://buzzplant.com/online-ratings-reviews-negativity-isnt-bad-think/

You Are Beautiful

Gabriella Iussich

Think of waking up one morning and finding dozens of missed calls on you cell phone and dozens of messages of friends alarmed because you did not answer for several hours.

It's late in the morning, you missed your job, and you don't really know why that all happened.

One of your friends finally gets a hold of you. And he is screaming, asking "why you didn't answer the phone?"

What happened?

You put together your thoughts and you remember that life is not so great for you at that moment and the previous night you thought that you did not really want to deal with your life the following morning.

That is what I had thought the night before and that is why that morning I did not really want to wake up. But I did. And it all started from there.

The beginning started from the end.

Paradoxical thing, but true. Probably the beginning needs to come from an end.

And the end is always the best way to start. If I think about it, I have a pretty good life. I studied for many years, I have a high degree and a specialization, and I am a good and respected professional.

That does not mean that I did not have some issues with myself and with the world around me.

I have a great family, but I think all started long time ago when I was a little girl.

Now I remember that little girl feeling a bit lonely, even if there was no loneliness in her life. She was surrounded by love and affection.

The loneliness was inside of her.

It was a feeling of inadequacy she had in herself.

She carried her feeling with her until that day when she woke up without knowing what happened. From that day on, that little girl decided to grow up, to be an adult. The first thing she decided was that admitting the weakness would be the first step. And she did it.

Then she decided to seek for help; professional and non-professional help. And that was not a failure, like many people think, but a gift. Yes, because even if you are at the top of the world, when you feel down, lonely or lost you have to seek for help.

And you don't have to be ashamed of it. As I said, it is from the end that the beginning arises. And don't feel you are weaker than others if you consult a specialist, or if you go back to your family to look for answers. I did. I went back to my family first.

The most difficult part was to admit that I had lost my track, that I was not the sunny and joyful baby they knew. But when I did, I felt liberated and free. And ready to start something new and beautiful. Trust me, I found out that when you let something out of yourself that bothers you in the present, you are ready to go deep into your past and find out what are the causes of your problems.

I found out that when I was a little girl I did not accept myself, just as I wasn't doing now. And at that moment of my life I wanted to starve myself instead of dealing with my issues. So in my adolescence there was an eating disorder that resulted in me looking like a skeleton and putting my life in danger. Well, one of my real good friends died for that cause, so there is nothing fun in starving your body.

My friend and I did not feel beautiful like the other girls. That is why we wanted to at least look skinny like them. So stupid and crazy. You are so beautiful, no matter what they say... that is for sure. And nobody can make you feel different; nobody.

As a little girl I couldn't completely understand the entirety of the issue, and it took quite a few years to understand the problem.

You see, even if you grow up, the problem stays there if you don't deal with it.

It can manifest as starving yourself, as a binge eating problem, as a drug or alcohol addiction or as a prescription medication abuse. That is why I am here to raise my voice – in order to encourage you, no matter who you are: student, mother, father, lawyer, doctor; whoever you are. Please take responsibility for your actions.

Understand your problem and speak up. Look for help and solve it, because your problem becomes not only yours, but also a problem for the people around you.

Don't think you are unusual if you have a problem. You are special.

And it is our beauty to be special.

Don't be afraid of finding yourself; don't be afraid of knowing yourself deeper and deeper. There is nothing bad in what you will find. Nothing.

I thought I was not worth it to go on. There was someone else who deserved it more than I did. That is so untrue!

Because of my profession, I have seen quite a few people leaving this life, and I thought: what are they feeling now? Are they afraid? Are they at peace? Are they seeing the light already?

Well, at one point of my life I realized that my life was important. Very important not only for myself but for someone out there. And I hope it is for you out there. You are not alone. Never. Not in the bad times and not in the even worse times. You will never be alone.

And even when you think you are at the rock bottom, think that you will bring yourself up and you will succeed another time.

I think it is hard living, but it is also a blessing. And that is all that matters.

You're worth it, just like me.

And this chapter is for you all.

Born in Vercelli, Italy, Dr. Gabriella Iussich specializes in radiology at the University of Milan and currently works at the Hospital La Carita' Locarno, Switzerland where she interacts with people from all walks of life. Having witnessed, first hand, the power of consciousness and manifestation, she encourages everyone she meets to believe in themselves and their inner beauty.

The Importance of Feeling Good

Monica Ivan

*"It's really important that you feel good.
Because this feeling good is what goes out
as a signal into the universe and starts to attract more of itself to you.
So the more you can feel good, the more you will attract the things
that help you feel good and
that will keep bringing you up higher and higher."*

Joe Vitale

The Law of Attraction commands that you love yourself first. Before you can manifest, attract, and live your best life you have to believe that you're worthy of it. This requires love and a peace with who you are and who you are meant to be.

Beauty is internal. We know this. You know when you look at someone who is at peace with themselves and genuinely kind and loving, they're beautiful. They radiate a beauty that cannot be rivaled. To me, beauty is the inner reflection of our ability to love ourselves (both inside and out). I see this every day when I'm working with my clients.

A beautiful being is someone caring, kind and loving. I think we are all beautiful in our own way. Everyone has a unique beauty; one that defines them and makes them who they are. It's very important to understand that you must love who you are. True beauty is accepting who we are and loving it. Each one of us is a radiant, spiritual being – beautiful and perfect as we were created.

Self-care helps us remember who we are and how beautiful we are inside and out. Self-care can and should take many forms. Body, mind, and soul... a balanced and harmonious combination of all three is necessary.

Self-Care for Your Spirit

You take care of your spirit or soul by having a deep connection and awareness of it. There are many tools you can use to create this spiritual awareness. Meditation practices also help you tap into your spirituality, connect to your higher self or your soul. Breathe deeply.

Other tools include practicing gratitude, journaling, and listening to your intuition and inner voice. I love listening to audio/videos of those who inspire me. It's also important to add that surrounding yourself with positive people and joyful experiences is great for your soul. Live every moment, Laugh every day, and Love beyond words.

Perform a random act of kindness. If you see someone without a smile, give them yours, compliment a complete stranger. The simplest little things lift your spirit and make you feel amazing. And who knows, you just might make someone's day in the process.

Remember that what you give, you will get back to you multiplied! We attract who we are not what we want.

Practice the power of gratitude! How amazing it feels to be grateful for everything and everyone that is part of my life! Every day I say, "Thank You!" I am grateful for being a part of magnificent Universe and love the beauty of life (with its gifts and challenges).

I think it is important to realize that every challenge has a gift hidden in it; after all, challenges teach us the most important lessons in life. They make a person stronger and it is a powerful reminder of being grateful for the beauty of being alive and part of this magnificent planet!

We often forget that we live on a planet that nature created so perfectly. Our job is to love it, respect it and protect it. We are part of this universal perfection and we shine the light within to make our days brighter because it is a reflection of our being, wonderful love beings with infinite potential.

Self-Care for Your Internal Body

You nourish your body by exercising, getting good sleep, consuming healthy foods and drinking clean water. Food is an important factor in our everyday life because fresh healthy food connects us to mother earth as we are one with everything. Massages help alleviate stress and tension carried in the body and let's face it; sex also helps release powerful hormones in your body.

Self-Care for Your Mind

We often forget or neglect this aspect of self-care. I value reading, learning from coaches and mentors, and by taking classes and learning new things. Spiritually, I follow and admire some of the most incredible people such as Tony Robbins, Louise Hay, Deepak Chopra, Joe Vitale, Wayne Dyer, Jon Mercer, Daniel Rechnitzer, Markus Rothkranz, Bob Proctor, just to name a few. It is absolutely wonderful being able to access tremendous knowledge from these amazing leaders. Taking risks and enjoying new experiences also fuels your mind and your soul.

Relax and care for yourself. Everything seems to be happening so fast these days! Pampering yourself is a way of expressing love, relaxing and giving yourself permission to reflect on how good it feels to take some "me" time. For example, light some candles, enjoy a nice massage, facial, watch a movie, read a great book or just do something you love.

Self-Care for Your External Body

Externally, you can express love for yourself by using products that are not only good for you but also make you feel positive and joyful. For example, a lotion that is made from animal products and chemicals may not be good for your skin or your external body. However, a lotion that's made from natural ingredients and is designed to care for you can help you express love for yourself and for the environment.

A healthy mind, body, and a happy soul – it's all connected and it's all an important part of living the life you want and creating your reality. The Law of Attraction tells us that like attracts like. By enjoying life and taking good care of ourselves, we connect with others at the same energetic level and vibration as ours. In other words, we attract people in our life that match our energy.

Everything is energy and we attract the energy that matches ours. That creates a power and unlimited possibilities. You can create any life that you desire. By focusing your energy on loving yourself, taking care of yourself, and believing that you're worth the life you desire, you're able to create an energy vibration that is ready to receive what your heart intends. Where your focus goes, energy flows!

Create your own consistent flow of positive energy. Establish a daily self-care routine. Create habits that support you to be your best self. For example, a quick and simple meditation routine every morning makes a big difference on how the day unfolds... or writing in your gratitude journal at night before you go to bed. You might dedicate a few minutes each day to reading and learning.

Love more. Researchers at Harvard University conducted an unprecedented study. They followed the lives of several hundred people for 75 years. Their goal was to uncover the keys to happiness. Not surprisingly, they found that relationships are more important than money or success. They also found that the closer the connections and social ties that you have with others, the happier and less stressed you'll be.

Worry less. In addition to loving more and building strong connections with those around you, the Harvard Study found that worrying about other people's opinions is a tremendous block to happiness. Instead, they found that people who weren't afraid to take risks and make mistakes were happier and more fulfilled.

There are any number of self-care habits that you can add to your life to take better care of yourself. The good news is that you don't have to wait for any magic moment and it doesn't matter how unhappy you have been in the past. You can begin to turn things around today. Your happiness starts right now and it all begins with loving yourself.

"The time has come to accept and embrace exactly who you are and exactly where you are today. Truly love yourself and realize deeply that you have great worth. Then decide and commit to heal past wounds, to do your best, and to improve yourself for yourself at your own pace every day from now on."

-Doe Zantamata

Make a list of ways that you can and want to improve your life. Choose one item on that list and take a positive step today to take better care of yourself. Integrate that self-care habit into your life and start creating the energy inside yourself that you want to attract. When you love yourself, you attract love. When you believe that you're worth unlimited abundance, you begin receiving it.

As an Arbonne Independent Consultant, I choose to deliver quality and work in harmony with our planet. I am blessed to be in a field that allows me to help others live their best life. As part of the beauty industry and a representative for natural beauty products, I'm can help others discover the empowering and affirming benefits of taking good care of themselves. We are meant to live a good life. Train your mind to see the good in every situation. Please feel free to connect with me at live.love.laugh.arbonne@gmail.com.

The Law of Generation: The Other End of the LOA Stick

Dana Lambrick

L ike most people on a spiritual path, I have my own "two-by-four story" – an incident that clobbered me over the head and forced me to awaken.

My sister had always been my best friend. As children, we were forced to share a small bedroom, but as we grew older, we *chose* to be roommates. As children, and later as adults, we lived together, played together, traveled together and laughed together...*a lot*.

When I was five months pregnant, I heard a knock at my front door. Beside my parents and two brothers stood the fire chief. All had their heads bowed with tears streaming down their faces. My heart dropped. They had come to tell me that I would never again see my sister. I would never again see my best friend.

After the shock wore off, I mostly felt anger – intense anger. What should have been a joyous time in my life was instead dreary, gray, and overcast. Most days I wasn't aware of whether the sun had actually arisen that morning, nor did I care.

One day, after having exhausted every avenue I could imagine to seek relief from the deep depression that had me locked in a stranglehold, I literally fell to my knees. Out of sheer desperation and concern for myself and my son, I earnestly prayed for the first time in my life. At that precise moment, I had a full-blown mystical experience, which included what I can only describe as knowledge being instantly downloaded into my head.

I instantaneously understood the big picture; the meaning of human life, my sister's purpose, and my role in the perpetuation of that purpose. Finally, for the first time in *my* life, life made sense.

I began a spiritual odyssey. One of my biggest breakthroughs came when I started learning about, and applying, the principles of the Law of Attraction (LOA). Over time, despite what I'd learned and practiced, I began to notice that even with all the awareness I had gleaned and all the work I'd put into expanding my consciousness, I was still struggling to consistently manifest my desires at will. Like most people, I'd often find myself sitting in the midst of some nasty muck, experiencing the complete opposite of my intention while I sat scratching my head.

As I stepped back and examined the bigger picture, I began to see that my overall track record for deliberate manifestation was not that great. I was manifesting what I wanted about 20% of the time.

After asking many questions, I discovered what was missing for me: I wasn't entirely grasping the other end of the LOA equation. You know, the end where I actually had to *do* something. Or more aptly stated, I actually had to *be* something that LOA can respond to.

LOA works—no doubt about it—but in order for it to work in my favor on a consistent basis, I needed a way to better understand my role as a signal so that what I was beaming out to the Universe was in consistent alignment with my desires.

I have often heard that human beings can be likened to both transmitting and receiving devices. But how exactly does this work? How do I transmit, and how can I ensure that my transmissions are to my liking? After more research and trial-and-error experimentation, I realized that ultimately my power lies in my ability to produce a feeling, which is preceded by a thought. It is my *feeling* that is being responded to by LOA.

In other words, whenever I prayed for something, it was my feelings or emotions – not my words – that were being answered. I refer to the proper mode for attracting what I desire (i.e., emanating a conscious signal and receiving back an echo that matches something I want rather than something I don't want) as being in the "tone zone."

However, I still found myself grappling with the transmitting end of the equation. I needed a word or a concept that was edgier, or more potent. To more effectively drive home this concept in my mind, I found that by substituting the word *transmit* with the word *generate*, I was easily able to wrap my mind around it, which is also how I came up with the Law of Generation. Everything suddenly became crystal clear. To me, the word *generate* exemplifies something powerful, like an engine, while the word *transmit* can be in reference to something that's either strong or weak (as in the transmittal of a weak radio signal).

However, I first had to *accept* the truth of my own power. Until I was willing to fully claim my awe-inspiring, innate power as the sole (soul) authority in my life, and accept full responsibility for *all* of it – the good, the bad, and the ugly – I would continue to create haphazardly, inviting all sorts of unwanted things, people, and circumstances into my experience.

Once I was able to see myself as a powerful generator, I began to dig deeper into the receiving end of the LOA equation. As LOA succinctly points out, thought is energy. This mental energy acts as the conveyer or the substance; the medium through which we generate and receive communications.

In order to become pure receivers, we must first become pure generators. Pure generative thought produces pure feeling, and pure feeling results in clarity regarding how and what LOA is able to deliver to us. Otherwise, our thoughts become convoluted, hampering our ability to receive clear, pure communication. We create interference by generating dissonant energy patterns, such as worry, fear, doubt, unworthiness.

The challenge is to generate a pure tone that matches your intention. In fact, nothing happens in your experience unless you first intend it to happen.

Is peace what you wish to experience? Then generate a tone that matches the vibration of peace.

Abundance? Generate abundant feelings and thoughts, such as gratitude.

Do you want more anxiety and fear in your life? Be my guest.

The point is that until you grasp the fundamental fact that you are the engine behind the machinery, nothing will change in your life. The countering effects of crossed wires and mixed signals generated by thoughts of fear and worry will most often override your intention for peace. The signal with the most amperage is the one that will be noticed.

The biggest difference I've noted between the average pray-er (someone who prays for something that is left unanswered or unfulfilled) and that of a true generator (someone who is consistently and harmoniously manifesting their every desire) can be summed up in two words: "ask" and "command."

To ask for something implies that you do not already possess it. On the other hand, to command a thing requires a state of knowing and of realization that whatever it is you're seeking already exists within you; all you need to do in order to receive the physical equivalent of your unrealized desires is to take a few moments to generate the tone you wish to be matched. Command it so, and then sit back and marvel at your creative prowess.

You are not required to ask permission. You can generate the frequency of joy right now, in this moment, as easily as you are able to wiggle your toe. All it takes is an intention and faith in your own abilities.

My life isn't 100% perfect. There's always something new to learn, an exciting, unique strategy to implement, or a deep-seated limiting belief to uncover, and I'm okay with that. The process itself is simply an invitation for me to consciously participate in the expansion of this magnificently brilliant, ever-evolving cosmos.

After all, what else would we do with Eternity?

For over 20 years, Dana Lambrick has studied everything from subatomic physics to metaphysics, and is constantly seeking resourceful ways to extract the nuggets of wisdom that are hidden within the very language we use to communicate. She's currently working on several books, and is creating a powerful program to facilitate a greater understanding of the vibrational keys of creation that are locked within the written and spoken word. She can be reached at Dana@DanaLambrick.com.

The Extraordinary Invisible Powers of 12 Highly Gifted Special Advisors

Ike Lemuwa

No nation waits until she is attacked before assembling her best and brightest armed forces.

There are two types of people in this world. There are those that believe they can, or should, do it all themselves. The other type asks for help. They leverage the skills and strengths of others and understand the power of a strong team. I can tell you from firsthand experience that the people who strive to manage their goals and dreams on their own often combat burnout. They make costly mistakes and they struggle more than they should.

Rest assured, if King Midas had a team and had asked for help or counsel, I'm sure someone would have pointed out the fault in his logic. True, Dionysus warned him to think well about his wish, but King Midas believed that he could handle it. He should have had a team of special advisors. When building your team, there are twelve key advisors to consider adding to your team.

#1: Praying Warriors

Studies have shown that prayer makes a difference in the health, wellbeing, and success of others. Thought has energy, and positive thoughts lead to positive results. Imagine the power that you can have when you have someone praying for your success and partnering with you. You're amplifying your thought energy and ultimately your success.

Imagine extremely gifted Praying Warriors who take your #1 concerns and worries, even your business, to be their hourly, daily, weekly and monthly concerns and solutions prayer wishes...

Ask 198TILG Highly Gifted Praying Warriors Support Team for assistance.

#2: Spiritual Counselors

The best businesses and goals are aligned with your personal values, passions, and beliefs. It's often a true challenge to build a business that continues to support who you are and your mission. A spiritual counselor or coach can help you stay on track by offering guidance and helping you do the hard work of creating a business that truly represents your dream and purpose.

Imagine A highly gifted spiritual coach, taking on your utmost concerns and worries, and making their #1 goal to fight your hourly, daily, weekly and monthly Spiritual Battles for you, while you go about your business!

198TILG Crowdfunding Support Team Provides Dedicated Highly Gifted Spiritual Support Team in 198 nations.

#3: Angel Investor Coach

An Angel Investor is an affluent individual who provides capital for a business start-up, usually in exchange for convertible debt or ownership equity. Their goal is to help you build the best business possible, and the assistance of an Angel Investor will go a long way to help you access emergency funds before you actually need the money.

When was the last time anyone ever told you, "Whenever you need emergency cash count on me, not your bank!"

198TILG Angel Investors Network Support Team.

#4: Personal and Business Credit Coach

Securing the right highly gifted Personal and Business Credit Building Coach will go a long way to helping secure your personal and corporate credit. Many people get into trouble when they're starting out. They overestimate their cash flow and can get in tremendous debt. A coach can help you stay on track.

Imagine building your personal and business credit, so banks and other financial institutions beg to loan you money, instead of you chasing them down when you are desperately in need of cash!!

198TILG Business Credit Support Team

#5: Personal Legal Counsel

Imagine waiting until you have a legal problem before you hire the right legal counsel! It's essential that you not only have legal counsel that you trust, but also one that is highly gifted. Securing the right personal legal counsel before you actually need them gives you peace of mind.

There is a saying that we have too many attorneys. Well it's sad to rush to search for one only when you're being sued! No one messes with a well prepared individual with a highly gifted personal team of legal counsel.

198TILG Crisis Management Support Team

#6: Ideas and Business Development Coach

You have a fantastic business idea. Work with a business development coach to help you optimize that idea. They can show you where your idea is strong and guide you to leverage your product or service to get maximum results. A highly gifted idea and business development coach can help you make your business success.

198TILG Mastermind New Product Development Support Team

#7: Business Legal Counsel

You've taken steps to protect yourself legally, now take the right measures to protect your business. A specialized advisor and business legal counselor can help make sure your business is protected on all levels.

In our society, it seems that everyone is looking for someone else to blame for their problems! Leaving your business without a highly gifted legal counsel is like building a huge mansion without a blueprint and solid foundation! Why?

198TILG Crisis Management Support Team.... in 198 nations

#8: Social Media Manager

Once you've built your business, you'll want to tell the world about it. Social media is a powerful marketing tool. It's also a time consuming tactic. A social media manager who specializes in building brands and creating awareness can manage your social media team. They'll create content, track results, and help you build a large and loyal audience.

As the saying goes, express love in many languages. Expressing social media in 198 nations is priceless! Imagine recruiting an army of extremely gifted and highly trained social media managers spread out in 198 nations, each crafting unique and rare content, promoting you and your brands non-stop while you go about your business!

198TILG Social Media Support Team in 198 nations.

#9: Reputation Management Coach

Today your brand can be built or destroyed in mere seconds. The Internet and social media have changed how businesses manage their brands and build their reputations. Hire the best and you'll never have to worry about your brand.

No one maintains a reputation if you absolutely have none!

Imagine engaging an army of extremely talented reputation defenders from 198 nations, crafting extremely targeted and relevant content to place you and your brand in the face of your niche community on an hourly, daily, weekly and monthly basis!

198TILG Reputation Management Support Team

#10 Local, Regional, National and Global Counterintelligence Coach

Your customers are next door and around the world. Your competition is also just as diverse. Today, your business needs to be able to connect with and market to people from around the globe and position your brand ahead of your competition, regardless of where they are located. A counterintelligence coach can help you position your brand ahead of your customers and firmly in the mind of your customers.

Yes, believe no one and trust no one! Retain extremely gifted local, regional, national and global counterintelligence coach whose responsibility is to make sure the product called YOU, as well as your brand, are positioned positively locally, regionally, nationally and globally.

A gifted expert must be in place to check and verify that your brand and/or image are being portrayed in an extremely positive manner. Blogs, social media and media opinions must be reviewed to ensure they represent exactly who you are!

198TILG Social Media Support Team in 198 nations.

#11: Public Relations Coach

Public relations is a part of a comprehensive branding and marketing strategy. It's also much more involved than simply sending out the occasional press release. A PR Coach can help you create and implement a powerful public relations plan.

As the saying goes, image is everything! Why allow someone else to portray you in the images they think and feel you should look like and/or represent?

Imagine the invisible powers of a highly gifted and extremely talented public relations coach!

If the media are not chasing you down the street to interview you, then you probably do not have a highly gifted public relationship coach.

198TILG Public Relations Support Team.

#12: Research and Writing Counsel

Content is the foundation of any successful marketing strategy. Between articles, blog posts, sales material, emails and social media you have an abundance of content to create. Content connects you with your audience, it builds on that relationship, it brands your business and it sells your products or services. Your content marketing strategy may be the most involved component of your marketing. Hire specialists to both research and write your counsel. Leverage their skills and experience.

When it comes to building your business and achieving your goals, leverage the skills and expertise of others. Look for highly gifted experts. Surround yourself with the best. Great minds working together can achieve tremendous success. Build a team of highly skilled advisors and be prepared for whatever comes your way.

198TILG Research and Writing Support Team in 198 nations.

The Ike Lemuwa Group, LLC and Mr. Ike E. Lemuwa believes in preparing yourself, your team and community for any unexpected attacks, any crisis, and more.

Visit http://www.ikelemuwagroup.com/ to begin building your team of highly gifted special advisors.

Mr. Ike E. Lemuwa is an American businessman and is the current CEO at The Ike Lemuwa Group, LLC, founded in 2008. Mr. Lemuwa is also an experienced fundraising strategist and Angel Investor who is renowned for his coaching abilities and his high level of expertise in the area of reputation management.

Whole Brained Midas Touch

Nancy Lloyd, Ph.D

H ave you ever had a great idea, invention or creation that was stuck in your head and you never "did" anything about? And that great idea you had… did someone else bring it to market months or years later?

Have you ever had a problem to solve and kept coming up with the same nonproductive ideas in your head and not solving the problem? And that problem you couldn't solve… did someone else come up with the perfect solution at some later time and get credit for it?

Those are examples of your right brain and your left brain not working together. They are actually competing with each other. One has an idea that is never acted on and the other has a problem and that it has no solution for.

Here's an analogy. Years ago I started having problems reading fine-printed material and mentioned it to a friend. She said she wore contacts and suggested I try them. Even though I was leery of sticking something in my eyes, I made an appointment with the eye doctor. After the exam I tried what he suggested and wore one contact in my left eye for reading. The doctor's office was in the mall and I was instructed to go shopping for 30 minutes and see if I liked it. I loved it for reading all those price tags, but was a little befuddled by the fact that looking down the mall, I actually felt a little dizzy. When I got back to the office, I mentioned the dizziness to the doctor and he said my eyes were competing with each other and would adjust in about 3 weeks. That seemed reasonable and off I went with my new contact.

It actually took 3 to 6 months of adjusting! If I really needed to see clearly when reading, I would just cover my right eye. If I really wanted to see the sign coming up for my next turn when driving, I would temporarily cover my left eye. Imagine what that must have looked like to approaching drivers!

I was determined to give my eyes the chance to converge into clear vision with things near and far.

What if your right brain and left brain are doing the same as my eyes were? The right brain is available to have great ideas (far vision) and the left brain is available for detail work (close vision). When they have not learned to converge on one point, then clear vision of goals, dilemmas, dreams, and every day events is not possible. Life becomes a struggle; frantic, fumbling and frustrating and an underlying angst that prevents forward movement. It is like standing at the fulcrum point of a seesaw. You have one foot on each side and are constantly dipping from side to side.

If you want to make life more fun, focused and fulfilling, and create forward movement, you must find the center or convergence point, stay balanced and be able to jump off the seesaw with a clear vision of your goals and dreams and a means of attaining them.

Just like many things in life, awareness and cooperation are needed to find that balance; clear vision and forward movement. In my book, *QUANTUM LEADERSHIP: Dare to See Things Differently*;

I share many stories, insights, and exercises to help others learn to create the changes they desire. Here, however, I will share something not found in my book.

First, it is critical to be aware of what is happening. If you find yourself stressed and full of anxiety about work or home events, you are primarily focusing with the left brain. You are bogged down in details, trying to "make" things happen and essentially looking at the world through a microscope. You can only see that which is physically right in front on you.

If you find yourself daydreaming, wishing, skipping work and/ or ignoring events in your day to day life, then you are primarily focusing with the right brain. You are "out of touch" as some might say. You look past what is happening in front of you and are essentially looking at the world with a telescope. You can only see that which is far away from you. The right brain tends to "let" things happen which is wonderful, but only when it is guided toward your desired vision.

To have a fruitful and prosperous life, you have to be able to blend these into whole brain convergent thinking.

Once you are aware, you need to start asking for cooperation. I know it sounds odd, but when you find yourself stuck in the dominant behavior of one brain or the other, asking for the cooperation of the other brain is essential. When I wanted to write my book, all the ideas kept me involved with the right brain, but until I asked the left brain to put some order to it and write it down, it didn't happen. When I was stuck in a problem at work and found myself frustrated, I asked my right brain for help in the solution. I then went for a walk in the fresh air to expand my vision, and within a few minutes had a solution.

The Midas Touch is the perfect convergence of the left and right brain, bringing clear vision to the goal of wealth with the touch of joyous purpose.

Midas was associated with greed, gold and riches in the desire for physical wealth – a function of the left brain. If left is the dominant force, it can lead to the loss of things that are not of a physical nature such as love, compassion and joy. But if you add the Touch of a joyful purpose, then you add the right brain with those feelings of love, compassion and service. This convergence results in knowing that great wealth offers great opportunity, and the ability to serve in love, compassion, joy and creativity.

Use your Whole Brain for the Change you desire.

Dr. Nancy earned her PhD in Transpersonal Psychology from Delphi University and has held leadership positions in healthcare related organizations for more than thirty years; coaching and mentoring others to "see things differently". She resides in North Carolina with her calico cat, enjoying reading, writing and the magic in everyday life.

Living in the Present Moment
Robert McDonagh

S ometimes I look back at my life and wish I had spent more time living in the present moment. I wish I had observed what life had to offer. Observed what nature had to offer. Observed what stillness had to offer. My life would certainly have been easier.

Your mind is a powerful tool when used in the right way. But the trick is for you to learn how to control your mind, rather than letting your mind control you. My mind controlled me for most of my life and the results were disastrous.

Paralyzed By My Thoughts

Looking ahead of me, behind me, and living anywhere but in the present moment almost wrecked my life. Truth be told, I had no job and no real plans or prospects in life. I was living on social security for some time, drinking quite often, and completely depressed. I'd lost weight. I had no self-esteem and suffered from crippling fear and chronic panic attacks. I spent my days in a cold sweat, afraid to eat for fear of throwing up. I had no self-confidence, no self-pride, no dignity and was diagnosed with stomach ulcers.

No one realized how much I was suffering. Everything and everyone around me was disintegrating, and no one noticed that I was crying inside. Friends would ask how I was doing and I would smile back (falsely, of course) and reply "I am fine thanks, and yourself?"

The Lonely Victim

During this time I also played the victim. Why me, I would ask. What have I done so wrong to deserve this? I was grateful for nothing, I had zero gratitude. I can assure you that this is a very long, lonely dark road. Life had backed me in to a corner. I wondered where to go from here? Had I hit rock bottom? Could it get worse?

I felt lonely, but not alone. There is a huge difference. Being alone to gather your thoughts, to go for a walk or to sit at home and read can be very relaxing and very rewarding, but the feeling of loneliness is a completely different ball game.

The Awakening

One day I went for one of my walks around a harbor and I just sat there. I was physically in bad shape, an emotional wreck and mentally out of balance so to speak. I was totally ungrounded. Disconnected from my true self, I started to look at myself like a third party. I watched my daily pattern and life. I started to rewind my past and go through it like clips from a movie. I was so exhausted from life that I just surrendered to this moment, to the movie of my miserable life.

As I sat there too tired to move and do anything other than review my life, it dawned on me. With sudden and sure clarity I realized that if my thoughts had gotten me into this mess then it was possible for my mind to get me out of it.

The awareness was so certain that I felt a deep emotional release all the way through to my core. I had goose bumps on my arms. I knew I had found the answer I had been searching for. I experienced a warm energy, a flow that told me with complete certainty that this was a true signal from the Universe. It was a knowing feeling; a feeling of relief – a feeling of surrender. Of course there was work to do. It took years to get me to the point that I am at now. I stopped being the victim. I learned and I took baby steps toward a better life – toward embracing the present moment.

I believe that there is no such thing as a mistake. That the choices you make in life are part of your path. They happen for a reason. You learn, grow, and hopefully improve. The years to follow were still a battle, a battle with my mind, and the demons inside. But at least I had this awareness of my mind's capabilities. I started facing the horrors that I'd been hiding from for years.

There is an expression "You can run but you can't hide." It's true when it comes to the mind and trying to heal yourself. The more I tried to push things away in the past, the more they haunted me; I only gave them more fuel. Now I knew that I had to face all my fears, and find solutions to conquer them.

The Tools of Living in the Present Moment

I embraced many tools to help me learn, recover, and stay present. I began practicing meditation, gratitude, and consciously living in the present moment. I changed my job, moved, and found new friends that supported my new life path. It wasn't easy but I knew there was no turning back. There are no excuses. When you want to make change in your life, you do what's necessary.

Living in the Present Moment is ultimately the key to your freedom. When you live in the present, you gain freedom from yourself;

from the false cocoon you build around yourself from early childhood. From the myths and beliefs that have held you back.

What is That First Step to Living in the Present Moment?

When I am asked how does one remember to live in the present moment, my reply is very simple. The moment you ask yourself exactly that, you're in the present moment! The moment you catch yourself not living in the present moment, be happy because now you're realization of not being in the present moment has just brought you back to this present moment right now! Eckhart Tolle shares this also. You can further connect with the present by grounding yourself and your energy. Sit on a chair or lotus position and let your bare feet connect with Mother Earth. It's a place where anxiety and fears begin to lose their grip on you, their power so to speak. It's a place of peace and serenity. Find your present moment and live there. Observe what life has to offer.

Robert Mc Donagh is a married man with five children who currently resides in Germany, Europe. Robert spends his time living day to day while helping others and brings to you only what he has experienced himself. Robert can be contacted at www.robertjoemcdonagh.com

Releasing Resistance
Henriette W.R. Nakad-Weststrate

This is a story about releasing resistance. When your dreams are large, you'll face more resistance. It seems to work exponentially. The larger your dreams are, the more people will tell you "no." They'll laugh, ridicule, and intentionally get in your way. It's not uncommon for the naysayers to win. Limiting beliefs, negativity, and fear all block the success of many people. What if the path to your dreams wasn't so difficult? What if there was one step you could take to make everything flow?

Starting at Zero

My dream started in May 2009. In that year I had a dream on the future of the rule of law. It came to me in a flash. Today I would say that I was at "point zero." The idea was just sent to me by the Universe. In my career I was often frustrated by the legal system. Court proceedings are time-consuming and take a long time to complete. People without financial means are often swallowed by it. They cannot afford the expense of years in the court system. Where is the fairness and justice in that?

This had to change. One day I received a letter from the public notary in my mailbox. I immediately thought about establishing a

130

private court that could issue enforceable verdicts by using a notarial deed. The verdicts would have the same legal force as the verdicts from the public courts. It is a very innovative, and complicated, construction, but the key was to make the court more cost-efficient.

Taking Action

The universe likes speed. When you have an inspiration as powerful as this one was for me, there is no room for doubt whatsoever. You only want to run with it. I didn't hesitate. Immediately after the idea came to me, I wrote a one-pager that outlined my vision.

I had but one desire: to make sure it was possible. e-Court, the first online private small claims court of the Netherlands was launched in January 2010.

Making Change Happen

At first, in 2010, I was so excited about the idea of equality of arms, that I didn't notice any resistance. Everyone was friendly to my face. Looking back I must often think of the words of Mahatma Gandhi: *"First they ignore you, then they laugh at you, then they fight you, then you win."*

For me, all and all, it was a time of positive energy, meeting lots of new people and having lots of fun. It just didn't occur to me that other people laugh behind my back. When e-Court really started succeeding, then the fight was on. Real resistance began.

Resistance Redefined

On June 23, 2011, I was invited to the Peace Palace in The Hague, as a Top 3 Global Innovating Justice Award Winner. Just before the ceremony, I was called by the Ministry of Justice and learned that e-Court would be banned from the legal system. This decision had retroactive effect. All verdicts rendered in the past two years were declared void. It cost me a fortune.

Normally, when you face opposition like this you go bankrupt. The Law of Attraction demands that you believe in your idea. You have to have faith in it and believe that it's going to happen – that it has already happened. My belief in my idea helped pull me through, as well as the support of family, friends and business associates.

The result was the unexpected. One week later e-Court reopened. It continued its work.

It was not until the end of 2012 that I understood that there was a "flaw" in the law that allowed court bailiffs and public courts to develop a type of "business model" which – in the eyes of many – goes against the general principles of good government.

Goodbye to Negativity

It was easy, during this time, to get caught up in the negativity. However, like attracts like and if I had any chance of seeing my idea through to fruition then I had to change my thinking. I had to stop disliking the people who were trying to kill my idea.

Instead, I wanted to embrace them with positive thoughts. I decided to stand above all the criticism. Step by step, I continued my path, and for every problem I found solutions. Again, it felt like the solutions were being handed down by the Universe again.

Positive Developments

The key to releasing resistance and realizing your dreams is to believe in them with everything you have. Knowing that your dream is powerful enough and important enough that the Universe will make it come true. Keep in mind that success doesn't always come in the form or shape that you expect. It might be different than you imagined. However if you're open to it, success will happen.

Like attracts like. If you embrace your naysayers with positive energy, they may come around. And if they don't, that's okay. The Universe has always its purpose for you.

Within only five years, e-Court has become the largest private court in the Netherlands. Even though it is banning the "undesirable business model," it handles more cases than any other private court.

The Benefits Are Far Beyond Your Wildest Dreams

There are lessons to be learned. I can share only one with you. When you have the inspiration, you can decide to take the action. You have the right to ask the Universe for what you want. In the meantime, be grateful for all the good things in your life. Then rest assured: more good things will come to you.

For me, the benefit of following that one short moment of inspiration that afternoon has been far beyond anything I ever expected. My life is full of passion and opportunities that I never would have imagined. So, embrace your inspirations as they find you, and don't be afraid to follow through. Your life will change for the better. The Universe guarantees it.

Henriette W.R. Nakad-Weststrate studied Dutch law at Leiden University. She was a lawyer at the Dutch law firm Nauta Dutilh. She continued her legal career in Banking and Finance. In 2009 she founded e-Court (www.e-court.nl). She is a Global Innovating Justice Award Winner and currently finalizing her Phd in law.

Out Of The Dark
Into The Light
Armin Nils Salah

A nother failed love story, and this time it hits me really hard. It is like I am repeating a pattern – different people, same story. I feel useless, unloved and unable to create relationships. I am depressed and unable to sleep, so I spend my long dark nights thinking about revenge for being dismissed.

By day, I am a successful manager in a multinational company. My ideas bring lots of money to the company. At the end of the day mostly all of the benefit goes to the company, and I feel undervalued and underpaid.

I spent numerous days drinking. Again a failure, I thought. Again the same story, and I'm so bored of the repetition in my life that I wanted to quit it. The only contact that I accepted was my sister on the phone, although she was very tough and direct. I wouldn't understand until much later that the fights with my beloved sister would save my life. She told me that I was creating all this pain myself. She gave me a book to read, Zero Limits, by Hew Len and Joe Vitale.

So I read the book, because I love my sister, and I realized that my reality was my responsibility. I had, in fact, created the unhappy pattern I was in. I began to take steps to approach everyone in my life with a more positive mindset.

I began cooking for people. I'd always loved to cook, and I realized that cooking is a part of my soul. As a boy I stayed in the kitchen with my grandma and my mother, opening pots and pans to see what was cooking inside – though my curiosity was not always amusing to them. During the holidays, I loved to help make cookies, and my biggest punishment after a bad grade at school was not to be allowed to create these sweets.

As a teenager I did three level cakes for the birthdays of my family, and as a student I cooked for my friends. Four months after reading the book Zero Limits I cooked a four course menu for 45 people in a restaurant –gourmets accustomed to Michelin star rated restaurants.

The joy I received from preparing this meal made me question my future. Did I continue on the safe path, or pursue cooking? As it happens when you pay attention, the Universe answered.

Unsure, I decided to take some cooking classes. As I approached the school for the first class, I felt goose bumps all over my body. I breathed deeply and tried to take in the moment, to increase the vibration. During this time of uncertainty I started a new relationship. It ended quickly. I felt like I was taking two steps forward, one step back. I realized, once again, that my uncertainty was getting in my way.

I set my ego aside and dove wholeheartedly into self-development and self-improvement. I decided to participate in a ho'oponopono seminar, I became a certified reconnection healer and I met Joe Vitale. When you let go off your ego and the attachment to the results, without abandoning the desire to reach your goals and to receive for what you asked for, great things begin to happen.

I did it. I quit my job let go of all attachments to a "safe future," sacrificed the person who I was, and decided to be a beginner again.

I enrolled for a place in the culinary academy located southwest of London, and owned by a famous TV chef. I thrived and am delighted to share with you that I did very well on my first exams. I am now a proud chef with the Cordon Bleu Diploma of Culinary Arts and my dreamgirl, Val, is going to marry me. You can live your dream!

How do you do it? How do you identify what you want, let go of it, and allow the Universe to respond? It's important to be precise in what you ask and wish.

It's also important to take action toward your dreams, interests, and opportunities. Invest in yourself. The investments may not always be monetary. You can invest time too, develop your goals, learn and feed your soul. Work to clean limiting beliefs and to create faith and trust in yourself and in the Universe. Take action when you're inspired. Don't question it or allow your ego to get in the way.

Don't blame others for your situation; take responsibility. And live the life that YOU want to live, not the life that your girlfriend, parents, or friends want you to live.

Find the tools and methods that are right for you. Maybe it's *Ho'oponopono, maybe it's meditation, or affirmations or praying. Find a practice that allows you to stay present and to stay positive and faithful. Learn to get quiet and listen to your inner voice* – Learn to trust that inner voice that guides you to your dreams.

When it feels good to you and your heart is happy and things are going smooth, then it's the vibration of this voice and you have to follow it.

When you are feeling blocked, see obstacles everywhere, or your heart and your stomach hurt, then that path should not be taken.

When you understand that you can now project in the future the creation of what you want, and when you become sensitive to your thoughts, you will make the right decision for you and your future. Trust that when you feel good doing something you love, you're on the right path. Take small steps and allow the Universe to assist you on your journey.

Having lived in Germany, Austria, Italy, and now England, Armin Nils Salah continues on his his mission to bring peace, and peace of mind, to as much people as possible by sharing his story through writing and cooking.

The Field of a Hundred Harvests
Ivan Nossa

This story is an extract from Ivan's forthcoming book, *Thank You (The Power And Magic Of Gratitude)*.

Andrea loved his granddad very much. He had grown up with him. And his granddad had taught him the secrets of the land. It was with him that Andrea first saw how a tomato and an eggplant grow. He learnt to tell when the strawberries were ripe and the zucchini were ready for picking. He learnt to love the taste of peaches, the redness of cherries and the sweetness of grapes. He discovered how to tend to the vegetables whether it was cold or hot. He spent many afternoons with his granddad after school. Sometimes he listened to his wonderful stories, tales and anecdotes. Other times they sat in silence, stroking the ground while being stroked by the sun. Those were the best times, the ones he loved most of all. It was then that he could feel the earth and hear the sounds that normally went unnoticed. He simply had to see his granddad to learn all that was to be learnt.

His granddad was also always so happy and peaceful. He never got angry. At 80 years old, he still hunched down in the garden to plant carrots. And when he stood up again, there was always a smile on his face. He never grumbled. This is what Andrea loved so much about his granddad. This is what made him such a special person in his eyes. His granddad was so different from the other people he knew.

Andrea would try to reciprocate. He would keep him company, telling him about school and the adventures he had with his friends. Andrea knew that his granddad had felt a bit lonely ever since grandma had passed away, and so he would take every opportunity to run along and spend some time with him.

One day, however, Andrea was unable to spend the afternoon in the vegetable garden with his granddad. Because of the demanding new Languages teacher, he had a pile of homework which took him ages to do. When he finally finished, it was evening, but his granddad had not come back. So before dinner, when it was nearly dark, he asked his mum if he could go out to look for him. He found his granddad lying in the vegetable garden, stretched out on the carrot bed with one hand on his heart and another on the plants. He ran back to tell his mum and the ambulance soon arrived to rush his granddad to the hospital.

He'd had a heart attack. Andrea wanted to go with him in the ambulance. His granddad whispered "thank you".

"Don't talk, granddad! You need to rest," Andrea answered.

At the hospital, it soon turned out that his granddad was seriously ill. The doctors talked with Andrea's mum while he looked on from a distance. His mum shook her head and then began to cry. He realized the situation was bad.

"Mum, please could I see granddad?"

"Madam, he can go in, but only for a few minutes, he must rest," said the doctors dressed in white jackets and with stethoscopes around their necks.

"Andrea, be brave, go and see granddad," said mum, who knew

just how special their relationship was, and went with him to the door of the room.

There was one thing Andrea had always wanted to ask his granddad. He thought this was a good opportunity, and possibly the last. He thought hard how to best ask his question, and what words to use. He did not want to tire out his granddad but he still wanted to know his secret.

It was a wonderful moment, one full of joy and emotion; they held hands and experienced together one of those valuable moments of silence that they both knew so well.

Andrea waited until the doctors moved away, then screwed up his courage and whispered, "Granddad, I'd like to ask you something. What is the secret to your happiness? You love everyone and everyone loves you too, even your fruit and vegetables seem to love you! Tell me granddad, how do you do this?"

"Ah, my dear grandson, a long time ago when my sight was better, I read something that I will never forget. It was by Saint-Exupery, and went like this: 'It is the time you have wasted for your rose that makes your rose so important'. Do you see? There is no great secret. It is really quite simple. We need to understand how fortunate we are, otherwise there is no point to living. Life is like a field. Like the field we go to in the afternoon. You can cast a seed and, if you are lucky, a plant may grow. Or, you can plant a seed, put down compost and tend to it with care. The plant will then grow better and stronger. And one day it will thank you and bear fruit. Life is the same. You can just live it. Or, you can live it and love it and be grateful for everything it yields. If you do this, your life will be like a field of a hundred harvests. It will never cease to amaze you and to offer you its best fruits."

These were the last words that granddad said to Andrea, leaving a great gift in his heart forever.

Dr Ivan Nossa is an entrepreneur, author, journalist, lyricist and songwriter. He's a certified Joe Vitale Advanced Law of Attraction Practitioner; and is currently seeking a publisher for his book: Thank You, The Power & Magic of Gratitude. Visit Ivan at www.ivannossa.com

The Importance of Understanding One's Life Purpose

Morris Nutt

M any now famously-regarded people at one time questioned their very own existence:

Moses, Thomas Edison, Albert Einstein, Henry Ford, Steve Jobs and the list goes on and on.

It is something that we as humans always seem to do. We have minds, therefore we think. We have souls, therefore we dream. We have goals, therefore we work to accomplish them. When these gifts of wonder and accomplishment break down, we then ponder why is this happening to me? Pondering then gives way to fear, disappointment and eventually the biggest question of all: What is my purpose? Why do I exist and what is so important about this journey we call life?

It is within this crux – this tiny sliver of crucial space in time – that we may then make a giant leap toward personal awareness or possibly fall into a confused state of obscurity. Everyone receives their moment. Call it a moment of destiny, a moment of truth or a moment of clarity, but it is a moment. That "pause and effect" of opportunity that you will look back on one day with pride or with disappointment. It is within this happenstance that you will discover who you are, what you are about and why you are here to make a difference.

We are all important. Every single one of us is a very important piece to the Grand puzzle. The President really is no more important than the best taxi driver. Here is why: the best taxi driver might be the one who delivers the most important person to their exact destination on time so that important person executes their destiny to perfection to further mankind's mission. If not for the taxi driver, the final verdict is upheld and diminished, and mankind's future hangs in the balance. While the President is indeed a very important and influential being, there are many mechanisms and safety net features around them to make sure the mission is accomplished. The taxi cab driver is paramount and independent on their mission. There is no room for error. This is why we must all take our "menial tasks" to heart and give them the attention they deserve.

We have been taught by many that you are only as important as what you make in dollars, and that you are only as famous as how many people know who you are, and that you are only as valued as what you can bring on some market for your name or your brand. This is simply a LIE. You ARE the following in any order you wish to arrange: **Important, Valuable, Wealthy, Wise, Talented, Smart, Courageous** and **Loving**. You exist, therefore your **ARE IMPORTANT**. And knowing and owning that very fact is what is so valuable to you and to the rest of the world – US. We are counting on you. We are relying on you realizing how valuable you are and giving this life your very best shot. We know at times you want to give up. We know you have bad days, weeks, months or even years. We realize at times you simply want to give up and sit down to not be heard from again. We know this because we are just like you. We also have wanted to quit and just die. We know what it is like to be stomped on and held back. We agree with you that it seems unfair and uncalled for. However, we also realize you are special and so are we. We know that if you give your very best, the rewards you create are well worth the effort. We also know that your life is just as important as any previous life whether they were a king or a pauper. We all have our roles to play, but each role makes the entire production come off as a success. We also know that we are all in this together and no one does it alone or makes it out alive. And because we know this very truth it makes us connected throughout time.

Life is funny, bitter, sweet and sad. It is like ingesting an entire buffet with one bite. Flavors of all kinds mixed together to form one giant gulp of wisdom, swallowed down together forming a life. How we respond to our destiny and creation is more of an answer than a question. The day that arrives when we "wake up" and feel our calling and know our purpose is a glorious trumpeting of reality mixed with potential. No different than a perfect glove fitting a hand or a mate matching your soul is the feeling you receive once you realize your true identity and your true purpose. I firmly believe that Babe Ruth knew he was a baseball player, just as Edison knew in the depths of his soul he was a true "tinkerer/inventor". Life flies by when you are busy being in love with your journey. There simply aren't enough hours in the day to do what you do so well naturally. And the rewards for humanity, not just for you, are immeasurable. What could be greater?

You may be asking what could be worse than not knowing your destiny? And I would agree with you. It is time to discover your real YOU! It is time for you to embrace not only your greatness and calling, but also to embrace your life path of enhancing humanity forever!

A few simple steps can help you in finding your real you. As Maslow created the basic human hierarchy of needs, you too need to discover what makes you "tick." What is it that makes you want to get up each morning? What comes natural for you? Are you an outside person or an indoors hermit? Do you like being very social or do you work better alone? Why do you enjoy sweets more than basic foods? If you were king for a day, what would you first pass as a law and why? These are very simple questions that will aid you in discovering very simple but most important answers about you and your Life's Purpose. In the end, these questions must be asked and answered.

Socrates had one of the most thought provoking and very best quotes when he said, "A Life unexamined is not worth living."

We are all counting on you to be the best bartender, the best farmer, the best teacher or soldier. We need the best of police officers and the best of citizens. We expect the best from everyone every day. We should also expect the best from ourselves. We are so worth the effort! The payoff is huge. It makes the largest lottery seem as small as a penny. How about a penny for your thoughts? What will you do with yourself upon discovering your Life's Purpose? Will you be so happy that you help many others? Will you discover a cure for life's deadliest diseases? Will you help the hungry and homeless? Will you help build a bridge that connects millions? More importantly, will you die with a smile on your face?

Now that is an important life. One worth living.

God Bless you on your very important Journey!

Blessings,

Morris

Morris Nutt is a 4x Best Selling Author, a Wealth Mindset expert and a highly sought after speaker. He is CEO of Morris Nutt International, LLC. He has co-authored best-selling books with Brian Tracy, Jack Canfield, Matt Morris, Joe Vitale and Dan Lok. If you are looking for improvement in your life, connect with Morris at www.morrisnutt.com

The Courage to Heal

Kimberly F. Oliver

I have been tumor-free for over 13 years. Did I have a secret? Yes, I learned it from being in the health care world for over 20 years and watching others survive and thrive. I learned it, and you can too. Taking control of healing yourself is a skill. I had to apply everything I knew to survive the softball-size tumor surrounding my pancreas.

As a nurse, I have seen life-threatening illnesses affect people differently; some healed and continued on their life journey, while others passed away. They had the same illness, so why do some people live and others fail to survive?

The answer is simple. How you feel about your illness and the emotional attachments you have to those feelings make all the difference. The energy and thoughts given to illness are there regardless. They can be negative or positive. It's up to you to decide.

Emotional Tornado

One basic emotion is felt time and time again toward any illness, particularly a potentially terminal one; emotional pain. It's common to experience a feeling of betrayal – your body has betrayed you by allowing you to get sick.

You may become attached to a negative vision of your future with your illness. It's not uncommon for people to dredge up painful memories of their past health problems and other times their body has let them down. All these thoughts prevent you from moving forward with healing. Too often people relish in the negative toward their illness. They want to tell everyone how sick they are, they watch sad programs on TV, and they ask themselves, why me?

I call this emotional pain a tornado. It whirls in your mind, destroying as it builds up intensity, and distracting you while stealing your energy from healing.

3 Skills on the Path to Healing

There are three basic skills that I believe lead to health and wellness. They include the belief and the awareness that you are not your illness, and faith in yourself, in a higher power, and in the people around you. It is the third basic skill that I'd like to share with you.

Show Yourself and Your Body Genuine Love

Loving yourself is paramount. Lucille Ball said that you have to love yourself to get anything done in this world. She's right. Love embraces positive thoughts, positive actions, and it attracts the best opportunities and people into your life. When you're sick, it can be difficult to remember this. You're full of fear and pain. Learning, or remembering, to love yourself erases the fear and pain, and empowers you to heal.

Create Loving Thoughts

The first step to showing yourself genuine love is to become aware of your thoughts. Begin listening to your internal voice. When you have negative thoughts about yourself or your body, stop and think about them.

Ask yourself if you'd talk this way to a loved one? Would you talk this way to your daughter, or mother, sister or best friend? If not, then why are you talking to yourself in the same harsh manner? If you struggle with this, consider hanging positive comments or affirmations around you as a reminder.

Avoid Isolating Yourself

One aspect of illness is isolation. Looking back, I do wish I had invested more energy into connecting with people when I was sick. I think part of me didn't want to be a burden on other people, and this prevented me from allowing people into my life.

It is not easy to be seen as weak, frail, and ill. The reality is that at one point we all feel ill. For some people it is just a week long condition, while for others it is a chronic illness. I missed out by reacting this way. I missed the energy these people could have sent my way. I missed out on allowing my church to pray for me. I missed out on allowing a support system for my husband when he was away from me and didn't have to put on his brave face. Show yourself some love by allowing other people to help you.

Give Love

When I was in the hospital I was unable to leave my room for a week. After that week I was encouraged to walk around the unit a couple of times a day. I will be the first to admit that in regards to my appearance, I am a "girly girl." I like my hair pulled back in my signature ponytail and I have a full ten minute makeup routine. It was difficult to leave my room with limp hair and a clean freckled face.

What did I gain by leaving my room and how did I show myself and others love? I was able to make eye contact with my caregivers, instead of them looking down upon me in my hospital bed.

I said hello and smiled as I greeted them by their name, allowing me to show love through respect. I was able to feel the confidence in myself by allowing my spine to straighten up and push my shoulders back. I showed love to myself by feeling confident posture.

It took time, and each trip out I showed more love. I would linger at the end of the hall and look out the corridor window. I would watch for something interesting to go by so that I could tell my husband when he came to visit.

I gave love by letting my husband know that I was taking action to improve, and this allowed him to relax and just be in the moment with me. Showing love allowed love to attract to me.

Final thoughts, do not allow your illness to define who you are. You are so much more than cancer, heart disease, or diabetes; you fill in the blank that applies to you. You are also love, love of yourself, recipient of love, and the giver of love.

I love you too, your body.

After, healing from a life threatening illness, Kimberly F. Oliver specialized in the human emotional response to chronic illness; introducing her to people with big ideas and caring hearts that shaped the person she is today. Kimberly is a member of the Texas Nurses Association, and Advanced Certified Life Coach for Myglobalsciencefoundation.org.

I Am Responsible for What Happens to Me

Stephen Oliver

Since we know the Law of Attraction to be true, it follows logically that we cause everything that happens to us. It seems to me that many people haven't thought enough about this, or taken it to its logical conclusion: we're responsible for everything!

Think for a moment about the implications:

- We're responsible for our failures. If you have low self-esteem, then it's because you believe it to be true.

- However, it also means that we're responsible for all our successes. Congratulations, you're a much greater success than you thought you were!

- There's very little in life that's random or arbitrary.

Of course, being responsible is not the same thing as taking the blame for what happens. It means that you've attracted, invited in, or even caused the events that happen in your life. All beliefs, issues and concerns in life, whether conscious or unconscious, have an impact on what happens to you.

In other words, one of the following situations will be true:

- You cause the events. Something inside you is at the root of the events. Beliefs about the world, and your place in it, can trigger events to prove the truth of that belief.

- You're complicit. Someone or something else is the original cause of the events, but at some level, you conspire with them so that the events happen to you. This is often a confirmation of some strongly held belief within you (e.g., "all men are bastards," "everyone is out to get me," or even "I'm a winner").

- You allow the events to happen. This is the path of passivity. For instance, if you believe that you aren't worthy, then you may let someone swindle you, use you, or otherwise cause you pain.

As you may have noticed, in all three cases you have a responsibility for what happens. Moreover, it's true for both negative and positive events.

I do have some caveats, however:

- You might be attracting these situations into your life because they have something to teach you. This is the basis for such proverbs as "as you sow, so shall you reap," and the belief in Karma.

- There is such a thing as being in the wrong place at the wrong time. The flow of life in contemporary society has simply put you in the path of bad events, to your sorrow.

- The opposite may also be true. You're in the right place at the right time, and you're in the path of amazing events.

Whatever happens, positive or negative, you should ask yourself why you were doing what you were doing, in that place, at that time. It may reveal more than you think.

How often have you played the *Blame Game* and put the

responsibility for the bad things in your life onto others? It's your boss's fault, or your family's, or the government's, or the rich and powerful; it's never yours. Or maybe you prefer to play *Poor Me* and be the victim, where the whole Universe has it in for you.

Hands up if you've played either of them even once. Come on now, be honest and raise your hands. That includes that little group of you hiding in the corner. That's better.

We've all done it, more often than we like to think. I don't know how many times I've done it, but the Universe does. It keeps sending me more opportunities to repeat the behaviour, because that's what I keep concentrating on. And it'll do the same to you.

Nonetheless, it's just easier to blame others for what happens, isn't it? You don't have to do anything about the situation, and you certainly don't have to put things right yourself. The problem is, when you blame others, you're handing over your power to them. **They** decide whether you'll be successful and feel happy or not. This is the way to be a vict*im* and not a vict*or*.

Even if you aren't responsible for the events, you **are** responsible for how you react to what happens. I've seen the word responsibility written as response-ability, meaning that we're all able to respond to situations. Your emotional responses, and what you do about a situation, are all under your control. And what you decide to do is the most important thing of all.

Do you panic, freeze up, or moan about how everything always happens to you? Or do you roll up your sleeves and get down to doing something about it? Whatever the response, it's **your** decision and therefore **your** responsibility. You're responsible for your *re-actions* as well as your *actions*! We all are.

If you're thinking that this is all little more than New Age psychobabble, consider psychoneuroimmunology, the area of medical research that examines possible psychological and psychosomatic causes for diseases and illnesses.

The results are fascinating.

According to the scientists involved, at least 95% of all illnesses and diseases, and 100% of all accidents, have a psychological element as one of their causes. If you find yourself suffering from chronic illnesses and/or repeated accidents, ask yourself how your state of mind could be involved. The simplest method I know is simply asking yourself out loud, "What is causing my problem with _____?" and waiting for an answer to spontaneously come up from inside. If you're open to talking to yourself, you may be amazed at what you discover. I know I was.

You're responsible, so you might as well own up to it.

You may be wondering where all this is leading. I know that while I was writing this, so was I. Then, last night, while getting ready for bed, I had an epiphany: If I'm responsible for everything that happens in my life, it means that I'm in control!

So, everybody repeat after me: **"*I* am responsible for everything that happens to me, so *I* am in control and *I* create my reality!"**

Now go out and do something about it!

Stephen Oliver is a Brit who spent over 30 years as a computer programmer and software engineer. However, he has also been involved in personal growth and self-development for over 40 years. His first book "Unleash You Dreams: Going Beyond Goal Setting" is available on Amazon. He is presently working on a second book about changing your life patterns into life paths, as well as a fantasy novel. He blogs on stephenoliverblog.com.

Exciting Life
Julia Beata Olszanska

Wouldn't it be amazing if we all were taught the Law of Attraction as children? What a difference it would make on our lives. The Law of Quantum Physics causes everything that you think and do, consciously or unconsciously, to come back to you. The vibrations are multiplied and return to you almost like a boomerang. When you are positive, you receive amplified positive results and reactions from the world.

I believe that The Law of Attraction should be one of the main subjects at school, because it has an important impact on our lives, our health, and it provides us with a path for our future. In fact, there are so many facets of the Universe and the LoA that we could learn – education that could change how we approach this life.

The Mind & Body Connection

15 years ago I had classes with Professor Emma Gonikman. She taught Integral Diagnostic Scheme. We learned how to diagnose the current situation of person's life; their Scheme. We could evaluate their health and how phases of the Moon have an impact on what we are receiving from life at the moment, and what we should do to achieve.

With Integral Diagnostic Scheme, we can see which organs are strong, which are weak, and how to strengthen them. We can also see the specific impact of our karma and how it is affecting our life.

A close friend of mine had cancer, and conventional medicine didn't know how to help him. He had a big house and he thought to sell it quickly to buy his beloved wife a small flat, so she could afford it. An elegant gentleman, he lived with his beliefs and habits. He trusted in what he could touch and smell. There was one "but"... He wanted to live very much! In his Scheme it was written that he should be a student for all of his life and he could always count on people who are very close to him. "Let's try to help him" – I thought. I had faith that we could help him survive and thrive.

We started from the affirmations and LoA, learning what are the most beneficial thoughts and words to use in our daily lives. We helped him embrace forgiveness, as it plays an integral role in manifesting a beautiful life. We also guided him on simple and healthy food choices.

He listened with attention and respect, but read and practiced by himself in secret – away from his friends at work, because they wouldn't understand. The process was intense.

What happened to this beautiful and elegant gentleman? He lived. He didn't sell his house and he and his wife are healthy and happy. He was able to return to work and has multiplied his earnings as a result of the Law of Attraction. As you might imagine, his newfound knowledge has made a huge impact on how he thinks. He now shares his knowledge and experience with others.

Everybody wants to be happy.

We all dream to meet our soulmate and a kindred spirit. We want easy access to healthy food and to be able to enjoy life. When you know and understand how the world works, why some have a lot of responsibilities and yet they are cheerful and prosper, while others are moody or always dissatisfied, suddenly life is a little easier – a little more cheerful.

In my experience as a coach, I have seen several lives changed. Some may call them Miracles. I believe it's simply the Law of Attraction in practice. I've enjoyed being part of many success stories.

A young girl stayed in bed for almost five months. During this time, her main nourishment was fast food, drugs, and alcohol. Her boyfriend did the same. She was in a very deep depression. A little coaching in the LoA and self-hypnosis, and this woman was able to turn her life around. She's in school, working, and loving her life.

Here's another delightful story. A 36-year old man helped people develop their business. He was well-liked, respected, and people loved him. He worked a full time job for very little money. When I discovered his possibilities we started to work together. Unfortunately, he lacked self-confidence. I worked with him on this challenge. In eight short months, he was earning 1,500 percent more income. His business has expanded and he's able to continue his passion for helping others.

If you want to see the world in full color, enjoy good health and wealth, but you're not sure what your next step should be, the foundation is LoA.

Learn how to use it and integrate it into your day. Begin understanding yourself and your reason for being here. What is your destiny? Why are your strengths and weaknesses?

Scheme of Internal Diagnostics is very useful to help you answer these questions, and self-hypnosis is an excellent tool to help change negative thoughts and a negative mindset. In record time it can eliminate barriers you don't realize you have – barriers that block you and make your life more difficult than it needs to be.

It all begins with knowledge. We're not taught about the Law of Attraction in school. We're not educated about the connection between our minds and our bodies. But it's never too late to learn.

If you're searching for something more than the life you're living right now, a Law of Attraction coach or other self-improvement coach can help you take the first steps. Sometimes all you need is a little help and some new knowledge.

Believing there was something more for her, Julia Beata Olszanska left her home town for London. Carrying only a few cans of food, a bag of sugar, and great determination. She now owns her own company, where she guides others using Law of Attraction and hypnotherapy. Connect with Julia at www.yourbest.media.

Creating Necessary, Meaningful and Lasting Change

Dr. Mary Ozegovich

Ahhhh! The Midas Touch. We all want it, wonder about it and maybe even dream about it. Imagine if you had the clarity, know-how and power to touch it, feel it and instantly enjoy it. Maybe we all do have the power or mojo to do so, once we are open, believe, are clear, and held accountable. Welcome to this chapter on Creating and Keeping Necessary, Meaningful and Lasting Change. I am Dr. Mary Oz and after helping thousands and thousands of my clients change and improve their lives, I am thrilled to have the opportunity to share some of the most awe inspiring and powerful information, tools and formulas I have used to help my clients. Not only creating necessary, meaningful and lasting change, but the improvements they want and need the most to make them the happiest and most peaceful!

Allow me to share a simple yet powerful formula I use daily with my clients to help them create change whenever they feel angry, anxious, bored, stuck or any other negative state and feeling. I am providing this formula and this chapter, which has been written to be interactive and experiential, so you can feel for yourself how it feels to make a shift quickly and begin to create necessary, meaningful and lasting change that you want and deserve.

Often my clients refer to me as a Change Expert who helps people quickly create life-long lasting change. When they first come to me they usually have a goal or outcome to reach, which is the easy part. I offer them some results-oriented coaching and then they are on their way. But the real fun begins when I challenge them to know who they are – who is their best selves and then help them uncover what they really, really, really want and how to keep it. You know... what they ultimately want that will lead to happiness and peace, not just success and fulfillment?

So take a moment and write down on a scale of 1-10, how you feel about a particular situation or feeling you have, or a particular negative state or feeling you often struggle with.

Write down the situation or the negative state and/or feeling:

_____

Now give a number to the feeling _____ (a high number like 10 represents strong negative feelings and a low number like 3 represents less negative feelings).

So, the truth is, whenever I feel _____ I feel like a _____! (Be sure to do this part so we can measure your shift.)

Here an example:
So, the truth is whenever I feel _____fearful_____ I feel like a ____2____! (Be sure to do this part so we can measure your shift at the end.)

Here is the **Dr. Oz Change Formula**. Read it first and then fill in the blanks.

Whenever I feel _____ (negative feeling or state), I will remind myself that _____ _____ (something positive and truthful that will make you more aware, more conscious of the truth).

I will tell myself with conviction _____ _____ (something positive and truthful that will help you move forward – hint: keep it about you, not others).

So I will now _____ _____ (take an inspired action that is connected to your two answers above)!

Here is an example for someone feeling anxious:

Whenever I feel _____anxious_____ (negative feeling or state), I will remind myself _____anxiety_____ is a negative state that can be changed instantly with a different focus (something positive and truthful that will make you more aware of a positive shift).

I will tell myself with conviction _____that I have the power and choice to help myself improve my emotional state right now_____ (something positive and truthful that will help you move forward – hint: keep it about you not others).

So I will now ___take a deep breath and refocus my thoughts on a more helpful focus and truthful statement, like anxiety is just an emotion that can be altered with physical movement, breathing, refocusing myself and certain coping skills___ (take an inspired action that is connected to your two answers above)!

Take a moment and be sure to fill in the above formula with a situation and or feeling you are struggling with.

Now I want you to take a deep breath and reread the filled in formula 2 times and then write down a number between 1-10 reflecting how you feel _____. (A high number like 10 represents strong negative feelings and a low number like 3 represents less negative feelings.)

Also take notice – has your number changed from before you filled in the formula?

Now I want to share with you the 4 Pillars to Creating Change. They are:

1) Be More Open to Change, 2) Believe Change Can Happen, 3) Be Crystal Clear about the Ultimate Change You Want and 4) Get Help and Be Held Accountable to the Change You Really Desire!

Picture a table with four legs being supported perfectly. Now remove one of the legs and watch the table collapse; watch the table fail, so to speak. That's what happens to us when we are trying to create change in our lives without consciously knowing about the 4 Pillars of Change. It doesn't even matter what kind of change we want. If we are not clear on all 4 Pillars of Change, we are not setting ourselves up to Create and Keep Necessary, Meaningful and Lasting Change we desire and deserve.

The truth is, not only are these Pillars of Change, they can also be used as 4 Steps to preparing yourself for the Necessary, Meaningful and Lasting Change you want. Let's look at each Pillar and take some steps together, right now!

Being open to change is all about expanding your thoughts and feelings to bigger possibilities. It's about moving out of your comfort zone, internally first and then externally! It's about opening both your mind and heart to the unbelievable happening. So whatever change you are wanting or dreaming about, just close your eyes and turn up the volume, see the change you want in a bigger, brighter, more exciting way. Keep expanding this image brighter, bigger and better until you have a silly grin on your face and feel that it is possible! (Using the example you gave earlier – see yourself being the opposite of what you were struggling with, maybe Confident – Calm – Self-Assured – Resourceful and Stress Free). Do this exercise right now!

Now that you are being more open, you are expanding your thoughts and feelings to the possibility of more, better, and who knows what could happen. This 1ˢᵗ Pillar can actually be Step 1 once you take the time and put in the effort to do the above exercise!

An even easier way to be more open is just ask yourself the following questions: What would it take right now to feel more open, and to be more open? Would now be a great time to tell myself that being more open can be freeing, fun and lead to great and unexpected change? And if you are really stuck with being more open just ask yourself: What would I have to think, say or do differently to be and feel more open? Still stuck? Ask these questions while thinking about someone you know who is very open, transfer their openness to you and let the answers surface.

Now while feeling more open, let's look at the 2ⁿᵈ Pillar and Step 2: Believing in Change. Believe is a very powerful verb. Let's just say without it your ship is already sunk. If you are trying to create some change in your life and you automatically think "this will never happen, this is too good to be true or this never works out for me," you have just poked a major hole in your hot air balloon that's suppose to help you rise up to reach your goal. Most people do not pay attention to how Belief is an invisible force that fuels change to happen. If you set two people out to accomplish the same goal, with the same resources and give them the same amount of time to reach their goal, but you infuse one with belief and the other with doubt, who would you bet your money on? It's a no-brainer: the man or woman who sets out to create change with a strong dose of Belief always moves incrementally closer to accomplishing their desire! Strong Belief is an inner sense of knowing that all is well and this change is going to happen at the right time, for the right reason, in the right way. Take a moment to think about how you really feel about Belief in general.

Here are some powerful questions for you to think about regarding your sense of knowing and believing in Belief! When I am looking to create change, do I check-in with my own level of belief? On a scale of 1- 10, is it low like the number 1 or is it high like the number 10? Ask yourself this coaching question: are there some daily ways I can strengthen my Belief, increase my Power of Belief, both consciously and unconsciously? When in doubt, practice being more open first, and then whisper to yourself, I believe, I believe, I believe, yes I believe, whisper yes, yes, yes, and be mindful of someone you know who finds it easy to believe! I know it sounds simple and silly, but go ahead and try it – just be sure to put yourself in an open state first and make sure you think of someone you know who is a believer (we all know someone). Belief can start small and grow as we see more evidence. If using the words "I believe" doesn't work for you, just say "yes, yes, yes" and notice how you feel! Then say "no, no, no" and notice how it feels. You have to admit, yes feels better, just as believing naturally feels better than doubting. Make a commitment today to work on believing more naturally and you will open yourself up to a stronger positive influence of limitless possibility.

Now picture the change you desire and just imagine how it would it feel to have the change happen? How would it feel to have that change happen now? Go ahead, read these questions and than close your eyes and ask the questions to yourself out loud. What would it sound like? Can you taste or smell the change? How do you look differently now that you are more open, believing and feeling the change? What are others saying about the change in you? What are they shocked and happy about?

If you are following along and doing the exercises, you are feeling more open and believing the change you desire is possible. Now onto Step 3. The 3rd Pillar of Change is Get Crystal Clear about the Change You Ultimately Want! Over the years I have watched endless clients never take the time to really figure out what they really want. Clients usually start their coaching sessions stating they want something in particular, only to discuss in the next few sessions they want this and that also. Whenever you want to create and keep necessary, meaningful and lasting change you MUST get clear on the outcome you really want. Do you want to buy a drill to buy a drill, or buy a drill to dig a hole or do you want to buy a drill to dig a hole, to deter the water from reaching your home and keeping it safe from mold, so you can sleep peacefully at night feeling healthy and whole. Which hole do you really want: hole or whole?

So let's revisit your original desire: do you really want to be less fearful or anxious or do you want to be super calm and confident, healthy, wealthy and wise? Is it your desire to have things, do things, achieve some things or your desire to be a certain way that's more important to you? Is it about having and achieving, or being, giving and loving?

In other words, when you decide you want to make a change, you want to dig a bit and figure out what is the result of the result. Do I want to become a best selling author, to sell my books, gain celebrity status, make money, make a difference in peoples' lives or to put my head on the pillow at night feeling accomplished, happy and peaceful at the same time, or is it about being, giving and loving? The trick is whenever you decide and commit to creating and keeping a change in your life, take some time to evaluate your desire, wish or outcome in terms of what are you really seeking. Just sit with the change you are seeking and ask yourself, what am I really after? How do I want to feel? Who do I want to become? What is my ultimate desire here? Another way to get in touch with your deepest desires is to set a timer for three minutes, close your eyes, put your dominant hand on your heart, and focus on your breathe in and out for 2-3 full minutes. Just keep breathing in and out, in and out, and when your timer goes off keep your eyes shut and ask yourself the following questions: What is my Ultimate Desire? What am I really seeking here and now? What would make me not only happier for now but for a lifetime? Go ahead, set a timer on your phone, put your hand on your heart, breathe in and out for 3 full minutes, only focus on your breath and then reread these insightful questions to yourself.

The last Pillar of Change is probably the easiest to do and yet the one most people avoid the most. The first 3 Steps are internal processes that happen within you: openness, belief and knowing what you ultimately want. The fourth Step is more external and requires you to get the help that you need and have someone like a coach hold you accountable to creating all the change you desire. If you research successful, happy, fulfilled people you will always find they never get to these great states alone. They have traveled through their journey of mountains, deserts, peaks, valleys, high and low places with fellow sojourners, helpers, mentors and coaches. The 4th Pillar of Change is all about being willing to ask for, seek and sign up for being held accountable to what change is important, necessary, and so meaningful to you that you would want it to last forever! In my own life, I have hired many well known coaches like Anthony Robbins, Joe Vitale's Miracles Coaching Program, Jonathan Budd and Peggy McColl to assist me in goals like completing my PhD, creating my own Results-Oriented Coaching Program, following my WOW dream and many other changes that I deemed worthy of investing in. In my experience, I have found whenever I hire a coach who delivers, I have never failed.

By now I am sure you are expecting me to ask you a powerful coaching question as I have done throughout this chapter. That's because asking powerful questions can shift you into a state of openness, belief and knowing. Close your eyes one more time and imagine the change you want to create. Make it big, bright and better than you thought before you read this chapter! Now see yourself as a believer and being supported by someone who can guide you, inform you, support you and help you avoid the mistakes, the costly habits and pitfalls that others encounter without a coach. See yourself creating the change you want and being victorious. How would it feel to be connected to a Change Expert, who is results oriented and has helped many others along the way? It's okay to smile, and smile big. See yourself being your best self, living your best life and sharing your best gifts! Wow, doesn't that feel good? Doesn't that feel right?

In bringing this chapter to a close, let's take a look at what necessary, meaningful and lasting change is all about! Should you choose to engage in some help and coaching, this will be explained and experienced in much more detail. As a Change Expert, I know that Necessary Change has to do with helping a client discover which two needs of theirs motivate and drive them the most. There are six primary needs that drive human behavior, which most clients are not aware of. Once a client knows and understands the two needs that are most important to them, they can begin to understand why they don't do what they plan on doing, and often do what they plan on not doing! Once a client knows their top two needs and knows what they want and why, we can determine their result of their result (what they really want).

Then we take a good look at what meaningful change is and what meaningful change they want. In this part of the coaching relationship, I assist clients in asking themselves the four magical questions on a daily basis, the million-dollar question and the multi-million dollar question. Once they have clarity we can combine their necessary change with their meaningful change, which is what they want ultimately for themselves and others. Then, together, we identify what it would take to make their necessary and meaningful change happen with daily conditioning. Daily conditioning is what helps the change become long term, permanent and lasting!

While conditioning the daily changes, the client is helped to also create a new identity of who they are. An identity that is congruent with their desired necessary and meaningful change as a new and improved Best Self that wants to be around forever!

Now take a moment and take a deep breath.

I want you to measure any change you have experienced from reading this chapter:

I now feel (identify a positive shift in your thinking and or feeling)

_____

_____about my anxiety, fear or whatever you filled in) because I now realize _____

_____ (fill in new belief or realization).

I feel like a _____! (fill in a number from 1 -10)

The truth is my number increased from a _____ to a _____! (Be sure to do this part so we can measure your shift)

Thank you for journeying with me and allowing me to help you create a shift, some helpful change and better feelings. I look forward to helping you in the future! For an additional Free Change Now Experience visit me at www.createchangenowforever.com.

Dr. Mary Oz, Phd is a full time Therapist and Change Expert who helps people quickly create meaningful and lasting change in the most important areas of their lives. She is a well-trained, educated, and successful entrepreneur whose passion is to help others improve their lives emotionally, spiritually, physically and financially! She resides in New York and is the author of several books. Visit Dr. Mary Oz at www.createchangenowforever.com

The World You Live In

Tony Perez

From a very young age, I have had an inner drive and desire to overcome and learn from the obstacles I have encountered along the way. I was drawn to challenges because of my desire to achieve and learn new things. I am not sure where this drive came from or how it developed. However, I have a belief that as children we are all driven to overcome challenges and learn.

As a child, your first encounter with challenges and opportunities to learn came from your direct contact with the environment around you. This environment became the basis for your challenges and learning experiences. Your parent(s) or guardian(s) have also developed a certain set of skills based on the challenges and obstacles they have had to overcome. This brought them to a set of skills that they passed on to you as a child. New skills continued to be handed down to you based on your interactions with those around you – be it your family, teachers, friends and community. However, because no two experiences are the same, you have also learned to develop additional skills on your own. The more you learned, the more skills you developed. These skills eventually became habitual and ingrained in your subconscious mind.

In other words, you developed certain behaviors or ways to act to given experiences and obstacles based upon your interactions with your environment.

However, as I learned through my own experiences, your habitual response system can only yield what it was meant to overcome in your past environment. In other words, it is limited to the set of skills you have learned. Therefore, you must continue to seek out opportunities to learn and develop new skills in order to modify your habitual response system. Otherwise, you end up in what is generally called "a rut." In addition, the habits you have developed subconsciously to meet with the obstacles you have encountered previously must continue to be challenged. If you do not challenge these on your own, life will challenge them based on the changes happening in your environment.

I've continued to maintain a desire to learn new skills, because I learned that the development of new skills and capabilities was the first step in changing my environment. As a young adult, I believed that this was all that was needed to change my environment. However, as I overcame new obstacles that challenged my habitual response system and older skills, I learned that this was not completely accurate.

As a young adult, I learned that you are also limited in and by the belief system you have adopted along the way. You have not only learned how to behave and how to overcome challenges, but you have also learned what to believe. Your belief system is the fence around your environment and reality.

Therefore, in order to escape your current environment and cross this fence, you must tear down the old fence and adopt a new one. In order to continue to grow and expand your environment, you must change the beliefs you hold. You must change and adopt a new set of beliefs that will allow you to develop new skills and update your habitual response system. Otherwise, you will be limited to roaming within the old perimeters and boundaries restricted by the fence you see around you.

You learn as a child to react to your environment and develop the belief that your environment is the predominant factor that influences your life and happiness. Some of us, as adolescents and then as adults, do not unlearn this belief. However, this same belief that worked for you previously is now the same belief that is limiting your growth and happiness. This belief that your environment is the predominant motivation for your happiness is the illusion that keeps you limited within the boundaries of your fence. It is not only false, but it is actually the opposite of what will bring you happiness. The structure of the system you have learned looks generally like this:

- Environment

- Habitual Response System

- Behavior

- Skill

- Identity/ Belief

- Universal Energy or Spirit

Consequently, you go through life trying to change your environment because you believe it is the predominant motivator of your happiness and joy. So, you buy more things, get into more debt, pay for more entertainment and distractions, consume more food, get angry at your environment, blame people, drink more alcohol, take more medications, chase more money, etc. I am not saying these things should not be a part of your life. However, you must eventually discover the underlying motivator to your happiness and stop distracting yourself with this environmental illusion. Your happiness lies in your connection with your spirit and the ability to change your identity and belief system.

I am no stranger to the system that many of us have learned growing up. I too worked on changing my environment first. But even with my innate drive to overcome obstacles and learn new things, I ended up exhausting myself. I climbed my way up the structure to the level of building a plethora of "skills" and capabilities. But, ultimately, I hit my invisible fence. In turn, I realized that I could not go beyond what I did not know I could change. As such, I limited myself to this self-imposed boundary until I looked within me for the strength to go further.

As I studied myself in introspection, I began to discover that if I connected to, understood, and changed the things I believed to be at the bottom of this structure, the items at the top of the structure naturally began to change as well. Consequently, I developed new beliefs through the repetition of thoughts, use of imagination, positive emotion and energy. In turn, those beliefs expanded my ability to learn new skills, which then changed my behavior and habitual response system, and ultimately the environment around me. In other words, I learned that the structure many of us have learned actually operates more effectively in reverse. Consequently, I implemented the following structure to change my life and expand my boundaries:

- Universal Energy or Spirit

- Identity/Belief

- Skill

- Behavior

- Habitual Response System

- Environment

My hope is that by me sharing this, you will also discover your inner power and use what I have learned to expand your boundaries and remove any self-imposed fences in your environment.

Tony Perez, JD, CMA, ACAMS is a consultant specializing in compliance and regulation of Broker-Dealers and financial firms. He also teaches audit, fraud, forensic and financial accounting for the University of Maryland. Tony also speaks at several industry and regulatory conferences. Please email him at aperez0007@aol.com for more information.

The Mechanics of Manifestation

Mirko Popovich

How do the multitude of events, circumstances and experiences in our life create a reality?

Where do they come from to manifest as life's experiences?

Manifestation is perceiving something through our senses that is recognized by the mind and noticed by awareness. In short, it is making the invisible, visible.

Whatever we don't detect, perceive or realize is not part of our lives and we, quickly and naively, assume it doesn't exist.

A deeper analysis reveals this is not the case, and provides understanding of this process.

Nowadays, many are familiar with concepts like: we create our reality; and what we think with emotion comes to be. "Like attracts like" is the basis of the Law of Attraction that has been sweeping the world by declaring, in no uncertain terms, that we attract into our lives whatever we think about.

We all have a Midas Touch but, unlike the unfortunate king of Phrygia who transmuted everything *only* into gold and almost died of starvation, our power is greater than Midas because we can transmute, knowingly or unknowingly, anything into whatever else we choose: gold, mud, despair, suffering or happiness.

We can know and understand why this is so, and why it cannot be any other way.

It's well known that everything is made of energy waves of different frequencies. Each frequency has unique qualities and characteristics when perceived.

Consider the energy frequencies range of visible light (Fig. 01-01).

We perceive certain frequencies as color red and others as different colors because our senses are receptors designed to detect and co-resonate only with a specific range of frequencies.

We perceive light through our sense of sight, other frequencies as scents through our sense of smell, others as solids by touching, etc.

Our eyes have three photoreceptors cones responsible for color vision. Each cone is designed to detect only one of the three primary colors (red, green and blue) that, when combine with one another, generate all possible colors. Each cone contains within itself the frequencies of its particular color range.

When we see red in a painting it's because that color's frequency is in the painting and within the red photoreceptor in our eye, causing them to co-resonate with each other – thus making visible the color red in the painting. It's the same for any other color.

If the photoreceptors in our

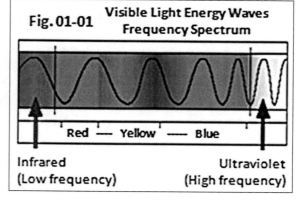

Fig. 01-01 **Visible Light Energy Waves Frequency Spectrum**

Red — Yellow — Blue

Infrared
(Low frequency)

Ultraviolet
(High frequency)

eyes don't respond to blue frequencies, as is the case for a blue color blind person, that color doesn't "exist" in our reality.

This works equally for all aspects of life's reality because everything is nothing more than combined frequencies, each combination determining and expressing its uniqueness by its composition.

This grouping of frequencies is called *frequency signature*.

When we perceive the white metallic cube A in Fig. 01-02, certain frequencies determine its color, others its shape, others its density and so on for every characteristic it has. Their specific combination constitutes the *frequency signature* of the cube.

If we change the frequency of its color to black we'll perceive the black cube B, which has a different frequency signature.

Altering the frequencies that give the black cube its shape to frequencies that form a sphere will cause us to perceive a black metallic ball C.

Shifting the frequencies of its metallic texture to those of rubber, and its color to white, we end up with a new signature corresponding to the white rubber ball D, instead the original cube A.

Another fascinating aspect about frequency signature relates

Fig. 01-02
Frequency Signatures

(Numerical values are for illustration purposes only)

A   Color: 430Hz
Shape: 346Hz
Size: 560Hz
Metal: 7890Hz

White metallic cube
Freq. signature: 9,226Hz

B   Color: 610Hz
Shape: 346Hz
Size: 560Hz
Metal: 7890Hz

Black metallic cube
Freq. signature: 9,406Hz

C   Color: 610Hz
Shape: 1246Hz
Size: 560Hz
Metal: 7890Hz

Black metallic ball
Freq. signature: 10,306Hz

D   Color: 500Hz
Shape: 1246Hz
Size: 560Hz
Rubber: 2890Hz

White rubber ball
Freq. signature: 5,196Hz

to "location in space," or locus. Yes, by changing those frequencies an object will be perceived situated "there" instead of "here."

Frequency signature doesn't apply only to objects. Every thought, emotion, circumstance or event has a signature determining its distinctive perceivable characteristics.

Frequency signature is a key concept regarding your manifesting capabilities because it constitutes the main determinant of your experiential and perceivable reality.

You too have a specific *frequency signature* resulting from the combination of your mental, emotional and physiological vibrations at any moment.

This is important to understand because:

Your frequency signature determines your uniqueness as well as your vibrational experiences and relationship with the cosmos.

The mental, emotional and physiological structures (Fig. 01-03) work and combine like the eye's three photoreceptors. Each co-resonate with a specific range of frequencies.

The distinctive combination of those three energetic structures at any moment constitutes your *active* frequency signature which, in turn, determines what you perceive and experience in your life.

You don't create or attract anything. You only perceive as reality

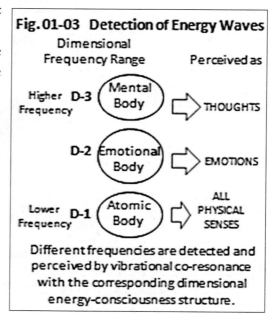

Fig. 01-03 Detection of Energy Waves

Dimensional Frequency Range — Perceived as

Higher D-3 Frequency — Mental Body ⇨ THOUGHTS

D-2 Emotional Body ⇨ EMOTIONS

Lower D-1 Frequency — Atomic Body ⇨ ALL PHYSICAL SENSES

Different frequencies are detected and perceived by vibrational co-resonance with the corresponding dimensional energy-consciousness structure.

the matching frequencies in the all-that-is of the cosmos with your active signature.

Frequency signature represents your State of Being which is the true definition of *feeling*. Feelings are not emotions, but the gathered sensing of the frequency combination of your thoughts, emotions and physiology.

Those three waves combine to form a *standing wave* which doesn't propagate but remains in the same location pulsating and radiating.

Imagine it like a surrounding energetic sphere – the bubble of your feeling and, therefore, the frequencies of your perceived reality. (Fig. 01-04)

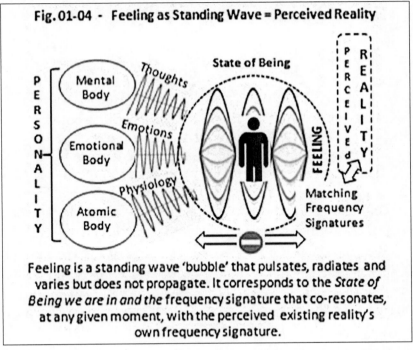

Fig. 01-04 - Feeling as Standing Wave = Perceived Reality

Feeling is a standing wave 'bubble' that pulsates, radiates and varies but does not propagate. It corresponds to the *State of Being we are in and the* frequency signature that co-resonates, at any given moment, with the perceived existing reality's own frequency signature.

It's important to comprehend that all frequencies that can exist already exist. That all frequency combinations or signatures of all possible realities that can exist do co-exist, simultaneously, right now within the all-that-is.

Realities 1, 2 and 3 shown in Fig. 01-05 exist simultaneously but person 2 will only perceive reality 3 because that's the one with similar signature B as person 2 has.

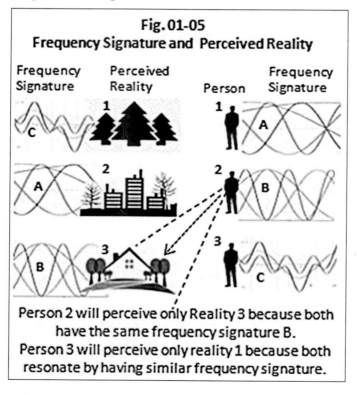

Fig. 01-05
Frequency Signature and Perceived Reality

Frequency Signature Perceived Reality Person Frequency Signature

**Person 2 will perceive only Reality 3 because both have the same frequency signature B.
Person 3 will perceive only reality 1 because both resonate by having similar frequency signature.**

For person 2 to experience another reality – like reality 1 – that person has to shift the signature bubble to match the one of reality 1.

Even more startling, if the signature of person 1 contains all frequencies corresponding to the signatures of reality 1 and reality 3 that person will, concurrently, perceive both realities and, therefore, be more aware while experiencing a broader reality in life than the other two.

Remember, all reality "signatures" you could possible visualize already exist within the cosmos, just waiting for you to tune in, co-resonate with, and experience it.

This is the true mechanics of manifestation. You create or

attract nothing in the sense of bringing something into existence that did not exist before. You only shift your thoughts, emotions and physiology of your active signature – your feeling or state of being. By doing so, you experience the corresponding reality.

You cannot stop manifesting. All you can do is be aware of what you're manifesting and change your experiences by directing your powerful Midas Touch wisely.

Find more about this fascinating topic at:
www.DecodeYourLife.net/midas

About the author: *Regardless of his daily activities throughout his life, like working as a software technician at IBM, a sugar cane and rice farmer, a builder contractor,*

establishing a toy factory or as a plain handyman, Mirko Popovich maintained, unalterable, his purpose of decoding and understanding his own life.

In his book "Decode Your Life," he shares his findings to unravel life's puzzle and explains how human life occurs based on well known facts in diverse areas of knowledge. Life, he affirms, has properties that are clearly aligned with the marvelous structure of the Cosmos. I like this being so, for I always prefer discernment, knowledge and understanding to faith.

You're Never Too Old to Learn

Marilyn Porter

I'm living to 100. How do I know this? My Mum and her sibling are now in their late 80's and 90's. I turned 65 this year, so with all this time left I wanted to make my life worthwhile.

Last year I went searching for a means by which I could fulfill my destiny. As the saying goes, you are never too old to learn. I have found through life that there are many stages in which you go through, and this was my time to do some in-depth learning.

I have gone through some hard times, which at this stage I can honestly say were of my own making. One thing that I did learn as I went through life is that when the student is ready the teacher appears. As we all learn in different ways, it is important to recognize the way you do learn. Then embrace it, no matter what age you are and know that your future can be an exciting and wonderful adventure.

Academia Puts Everyone in a Box

When I was young I had difficulty learning. I remember that one of the teachers at school told my Mum & Dad if he could hold my attention in the classroom long enough, I would learn. But

I was a dreamer, so my mind was not on the teacher but out the window on some wild adventure.

I then believed that I was dumb, stupid, that I didn't have the ability to learn. Fear settled in and the belief in me grew. The fear was so strong that I never completed my final year at school.

It wasn't until I was in my 30's that I started to realize that I wasn't stupid. I simply did things differently. We are not all the same, we all learn differently.

Seminars are a great way in which to learn. Interacting with others is a great help, and the hands on practice in my chosen field is so beneficial to me. It is important to find out your passion and follow through with it.

As a result of all the counseling that I had over the years, I did courses in Hypnotherapy, Lifeline telephone counseling, Alpha Dynamics, Mind Mastery and many more. My goal was to help others, but somewhere deep inside myself I still believed that I wasn't good enough.

An event at the end of 2012 made me start questioning myself. I was angry that I had been so stupid. I was also trying to sort out my relationship with my four children, which I felt I had neglected. I needed answers, and the search took me to a seminar in Queensland. This was the beginning of 2013.

At this seminar there were three powerful women: Cyndi O'Meara, a Nutritionist; Kim Morrison, of Pure Natural Oils; and Carren Smith, who survived the Bali Bombing and wrote a book "Soul Survivor." I also participated in a Manifesting Course in Greece with Dr Michelle Neilson, author of "Manifesting Matisse".

My life was changing. I went searching for a modality that would suit me. While searching on the Web I came across a site called FasterEFT. I went onto YouTube, where Robert G. Smith, creator of FasterEFT, had over 600 videos. I started to watch the videos and worked on myself. At the end of October 2013 I bought the Kit. I am now a FasterEFT Level III practitioner.

Clearing Must Come First

Clearing is a process of getting rid of the beliefs and thoughts that hold you back. We cannot change the past, but we can change our perception about the events of the past. For example, I wasn't able to embrace learning until I let go of my belief that I was stupid. Through this process I have let go of the old belief and formed a new one, I am great.

FasterEFT is one method of clearing these programs quickly and efficiently. There are many different modalities out there that can help you heal. You can overcome your past and move forward with your life in a positive and productive way. You're never too old to learn, change, grow, and prosper. Age doesn't matter.

Find Leaders and Teachers That Are Right for You

After years of learning, growing, and working on myself, I'd messed up again. I'd done something that made me simply furious with myself. Like an onion, there are many layers, so as we peel one layer off, another is revealed. What is really interesting is the changes that are made today will reflect the person you truly are and change all your tomorrows.

You're ready to change how you think and you're ready to begin letting go of your programming; the Universe delivers profound messages to you. It places teachers in your path.

I have learnt from many teachers over the last 12 months. Of course, my biggest teacher to date is Robert G. Smith, creator of FasterEFT.

Many years ago I watched "The Secret," and I first saw Joe Vitale. Joe is one of the people I follow through emails, and I have also read several of his books. All of this has helped me on my journey. Dr Hew Len, co-author of the book Zero Limits, and Teacher of Ho'oponopono is another great teacher.

There have been many good teachers over the years, to name just some of them: Zig Ziglar, Bob Proctor, Wayne Dwyer, Anthony Robbins, Louise L. Hay, and recently Igor Ledochowski (Hypnotherapist), Morry Zelcovitch (Quantum Mind Power), Winter Vee, Steve G. Jones and many, many more.

When you are ready to release your Fears and Emotions, Life becomes an open book to the new you. Find the passion inside of you and follow your dreams. The most important thing in life, I believe, is Love; first of all you must Love yourself Unconditionally. You can change your life, and open yourself up to a whole new world.

Marilyn Joan Porter, an Australian Aboriginal, Level III FEFT practitioner, Certified Conversational Hypnotherapist, Lifeline Certificate III Telephone Counsellor. I have four beautiful children & seven gorgeous grandchildren. I work with people all over the world through Skype. Find out more on www.healingbyfastereft.com. I hold seminars to promote my business.

The Power of Choice
Sarah Sanchez

Choice is defined by Merriam-Webster's dictionary as "the act of choosing: the act of picking or deciding between two or more possibilities." If you look at that definition on paper, it seems pretty simple, right? We wake up, check the time, decide if it's going to be "coffee and a bagel" or "grab the keys and forget food" kind of morning. We are always in a state of simple and not-so-simple decision making modes. Sometimes the easiest choice can leave us powerless, or it can inspire us and those close enough to us to feel fulfilled.

My experience with choice has been an interesting one. I've made my fair share of great decisions, as well as many others that were just poor and tasteless. I grew up in a fairly conservative Roman Catholic household, went to Catholic grade school and after graduating high school I paid my way for college through my service with the U.S. Army National Guard. I had a great childhood, full of laughs, supportive family and friends, and got to experience many things and see places on this earth that many will never have the opportunity to see.

Some of my most memorable moments happened in the

military. Being promoted right before a huge deployment and meeting some of the most courageous people on the face of the planet are just two. Growing up in all of these traditional norms did nothing for me when it came to handling "life after death" situations – something I had no real experience in.

In 2007, after coming home from my deployment to Iraq I drank and smoked the pain away. I was diagnosed with PTSD by the Department of Veterans Affairs. I was lying to my therapists about how well I was doing, and then going home to sleep for 12-18 hours a day. They put me on prescriptions that were clearly labeled "not to be consumed with alcohol." My addictions were all over the place. Sleep, drink, smoke here and there. I spiraled and somehow was able to hide enough to get by from those who actually cared. I only showed my surface. When I would have friends visit I would leave very little room for talk of happiness and joy that I once had in my life. I took people and things that would come into my life for granted. I thought the world owed me something because of a service I chose to get into. Wait, a second...

I CHOSE THIS!

Crazy, right?! I mean who does this? Who chooses to put themselves so far out there that they are willing to give their life for it? Answer: ME. I did. The choices I made led me to where I was in that point in my life. So, what did I do about it?

Well, for a few years (three to be exact) I ignored it. I was so set in my mind that no one and nothing was going to change this being I had become after doing a great service to the nation I was born to. Take a wild guess where that got me. I drank on occasion to forget things selectively. If I had a bad day at work I took it out at home (nothing like bringing work issues home, right?). I kept finding myself doing jobs that I couldn't stand when I knew damned well I had more potential and energy to give the world. I had a ton of regrets and mounting mental health issues according to my doctors. I took all those "truths" to be my life whilst forgetting one major factor: choice.

Often times we get so involved in our everyday affairs (occasionally with good reason) that we forget about what counts the most. After all the turmoil in my head, and living out the prophecies that therapists and doctors had given me, I realized it was time for some major changes. At the rate I was going I was told to expect diabetes and heart conditions by age 45. Don't get me wrong, doctors and therapists have very difficult jobs and work very well every day to help patients in need, but what I needed couldn't be found in any office. My family was very open and helpful in all the ways they could be. But they really weren't sure what to do, nor did they have any experience with a young woman who had a very "loose cannon" attitude as well as mental health issues. This is the part where things got very exciting and scary all at the same time.

I realized that by changing what I thought throughout my days, I could change my life back to wellness. Now, I didn't do this alone and I'm not trying to make it sound as if this was an easy process. It's not. Humans have been doing this for centuries. What I chose to do was live my TRUTH. I put in my retirement packet with the National Guard to medically retire. I visualized them approving and shortly thereafter it was granted. I am 33 years old. I don't know any of my friends in this position let alone some of the people I know over 60. I made a choice, and I actively make them every day to be well.

I said to myself that I need to deal with ALL of my issues (and I mean ALL) in order to get to where I am going. Living your truth is a liberating feeling. It's one of the most terrifying choices you will make in your life. It has to start with YOU. You are the only one who has the power to do this. The only thing that holds you back is you! Make it your life no matter the circumstance and you will see the change. Don't let another person's truth start to reflect in your life unless you want to live in someone else's shoes.

Love, Light and Happiness,
Sarah

Sarah M. Sanchez was born and raised in Chester County, Pennsylvania. She was deployed to Iraq in 2006. After coming home and being diagnosed with PTSD she persevered and graduated from West Chester University in 2011. Sarah's current passion is assisting others with the struggles of PTSD.

A Dream Deferred
Rev. Maureen Shelly-Burns

I believe that any life, any situation, can be transformed, no matter how bad it seems. I know this in my heart and soul. I know this from experience having been a victim of gang rape while I served in the Army. I suffered from PTSD, depression and substance abuse. It got so bad that I even tried to take my life. I eventually suffered a nervous breakdown and then I made a choice.

I am a walking, breathing and loving example that anyone can overcome trauma. Anyone can live a life of abundance, and they can learn to manifest their dreams and desires. You can learn to let go of and clear limiting beliefs and paradigms. You can overcome anything.

You can take the long slow path to a better life, or you can take a shortcut. Why wouldn't you want to start living your dream life as soon as possible?

What is the fast track to happiness? Finding a mentor or coach can make a dramatic difference in your life. I found solutions, but it took me many years to get to a good place. If I'd sought out the help of a mentor or coach, I could have reached this place of abundance and happiness much sooner.

Here are a few essential keys to success.

Find faith, believe. With God, you can always have a second chance at a first-rate life. The biblical story of Job proves this point. Job lost everything except his faith in God, and all was restored to him and more. I filed a lawsuit against the Army for PTSD. I prayed for 10 years to win my case. I never gave up and in the end justice prevailed.

All things are possible with the help of a Higher Power. Once we learn how to practice Law of Attraction principles, the Universe supports the shift in energy. All you have to do is ask and receive, like in the story of Aladdin's lamp.

Law of Attraction methods have radically transformed my life. I have manifested over $100,000 from my lawsuit settlement, tripled my income, bought a new car for cash, bought my first home and married my soulmate. All in my 50s.

Experience gratitude. Gratitude is necessary to the process of living a life of abundance. Learn to practice it daily. Keeping a gratitude journal is a simple practice that can make a dramatic difference in your life.

Forgive. Forgiving yourself and others is absolutely necessary to overcoming trauma. This has taken me a lifetime to learn. Without forgiveness, we stay stuck in a never-ending cycle. Your world is filled with resentments, shame and blame. With forgiveness, you can learn to trust your instincts and, as Oprah Winfrey says, "Follow your instincts. That's where true wisdom manifests itself."

Seek and embrace support. You have to learn to accept and embrace where you are now if you want to move forward. We don't live in isolation. In fact, people – especially those suffering from trauma and PTSD – can and do die from just that. You need the help of friends and family, or community, and most importantly, you need to develop a relationship with a Higher Power. During my assault, I vowed that if I lived through it, I would serve God for the rest of my life. I have kept that promise and honored my vow.

There is help out there. You just need to look for it. Gratitude and forgiveness are essential for transformation. Developing a relationship with a Higher Power is vital. The process of recreation is not a one man job. You need to be open to finding a mentor or coach.

I also used Creative Reinvention, a powerful book by Elaine Shelly which describes four steps in detail. The 1ˢᵗ step is Choose, which means make a conscious choice to change and be happy. Decide, Plan and Act are the other steps further outlined in her book. Creative Reinvention is a process. These steps are solid principles for positive and lasting change. You're in control. You get to decide when to be happy.

Believe that you can recreate your life by being willing to take the necessary steps to manifest a life filled with abundance. And don't go it alone. Find a coach or mentor and reach out.

Lastly, I would like to recommend the use of the Serenity Prayer, which I have practiced for over 30 years. At first I would just recite it. Now I live by it.

"God grant me the serenity to accept the things I cannot change the courage to change the things I can and the wisdom to know the difference."

Blessings on your journey.

Rev. Maureen Shelly-Burns is an Advanced Practitioner Law of Attraction coach. Since 1999 Maureen has served as a minister at City of Refuge UCC in Oakland California. She believes faith inspires and supports manifestation principles. For a coaching consultation contact Maureen at transformationspossible.com

Determination
Is Not Enough
Sara Tawata-Min

I was born and raised in Peru and arrived in the United States unable to speak English. I didn't have any money, and was not able to purchase things on credit because I had none. I only had what I was able to bring with me, and the help of my sister.

In Peru I was educated and worked as a dentist, and but upon arrival and over the next few years went through the process of learning English and getting licensed in the U.S.

I've spent much of my life functioning from a place of trust and determination. I wanted to move to the U.S., I did. I wanted to practice dentistry, I am. I wanted to attract a husband and kids and I did. I didn't have a formal Law of Attraction practice; I didn't even know what it was. What I had initially was an intense drive and the faith that I would achieve my goals.

I started working right after I became a licensed dentist. Just a few short months after I began working at the practice, the doctor I was working for offered to sell me the practice. In spite of some challenges I was able to figure things out and in the end was able to buy the practice! I was determined.

But determination without faith won't get you far enough. You have to pay attention to the signs. You have to be aware and take action. I've always been a positive person, but I was unfamiliar with the Law of Attraction until my brother introduced me to The Secret, and then my quest for knowledge took off.

That is when I realized that anything is possible. I started learning about the Law of Attraction, reading books, listening to audio recordings, getting coaching, attending seminars, etc. All that knowledge gave me the certainty to know where I am going, to what I really want; to a happy life. Granted, I didn't know how it was going to play out, but I knew the Universe would show me.

Practicing the Law of Attraction has become part of my daily life. I am teaching my children to practice gratitude, to clean their limiting beliefs and thoughts, and to embrace positive affirmations. These practices make a difference, I can tell. They can see life in a different way, with a different mirror.

By eliminating the negative beliefs that were holding me back, and by embracing the present and being grateful for it, I am able to actually help other people. I've shared what I know with my staff and it has made a big difference. The employees are happier. They smile, they don't complain and criticize like they used to, and instead we laugh together. We really do enjoy working together.

Even our patients can see the difference. It is amazing to see how many people open up to us, people that we don't really know start telling us their stories. It is nice to feel that they really appreciate us like a family. They like to come to the dentist, which is a miracle all by itself. Sometimes we even have patients just stop by to say "hi" or bring goodies.

You can attract wonderful things into your life by practicing the Law of Attraction in a proper way and taking action on it. However if you don't let go of negativity, and don't get rid of your limiting beliefs and fears, then that's what you are going to be attracting. We have to learn to embrace the moment, have positive mindset, and be grateful. My life has changed so much for the better. Practicing the Law of Attraction puts all my goals and desires in alignment.

If you want to do it, there is always a way, you just have to figure out the how and to trust that the Universe will provide. Before, I didn't understand know how the universe worked. Now I understand that miracles happen and they happen all the time. The answers are constantly flashing by our eyes. Our responsibility is to clear ourselves and all the old programming so we are able to see them. It is a daily task to clear our minds, like taking a shower.

So, the real secret is to live the present, be aware and be grateful! Have a wonderful life!

Born in Lima, Peru, Sara Tawata-Min moved to the U.S. in 1999. Determined to make a great life for herself, she married and began practicing dentistry in 2003. Realizing that determination was only half of the success equation, she began studying and practicing the Law of Attraction. Dr. Tawata-Min now uses the LoA to help others improve their lives.

Voted best dental practice in The Santa Maria Sun, you can visit Dr. Sara Tawata-Min at santamariatowncenterdental.com.

The Golden Ice-Cream
Ricardo Torres

How many successful people would you say knew from the beginning which would be the path to achieving their goals? I could say with a high degree of certainty that none of them knew. So what did they do in order to get to the place they wanted to be in life?

Well, we can say that regarding manifestation there is a receptive part – in which you get to go to the places you want to, people come into your life, you buy the car that you like, or the house of your dreams, etc. That's what we focus on when we visualize the life that we wish; we imagine ourselves in a scenario of receiving all the goods of life and we often think that's all we have to do when we talk about Law of Attraction.

While that may be true, there is one more side, which is not about receiving, but about creating, about taking action. That's the expressive part of manifestation that many people miss. We constantly receive ideas and inspiration to do things; write that book, initiate that project, start a business, and most of the times, it remains only that; an idea. Even if we like it, we don't express it because of fear; dismissing its possible success, and for many other reasons that just inhibit us from taking action and bringing that thing that exists only in our minds to reality. These ideas could be the vehicle to achieve one of our goals, and initiate a chain of golden miracles in our lives through changing whatever may be blocking us, whether that's our thoughts, emotions or lack of action.

Let me tell you a personal experience. A few years ago I was in Europe, a dream I could accomplish through inspiration. I made the trip with my life's savings and I had no job at that moment, so that was all the money I had left. I was going to stay 3 months and I only knew that I wanted to have a lot of great experiences in that adventure.

Somewhere around the second week, I got the urge to buy an ice cream – you might say I was inspired to do so – as it cost less than 1 euro. But, as you may have felt in your life, fear arises when we less expect it. I had thoughts and emotions about the scarcity of money and its permanence in my life... and remember that this is for spending less than 1 euro. I was feeling the negative emotion, thinking that I should save as much money as I could so that I would be able to spend it in the really big important experiences that could take place with the people I could get to meet.

Fortunately, the light found its place, I began to relax, and I realized that the only real guide that I had for the amazing friendships and experiences I wanted to have was what I could receive from my inner voice and to follow it. So, I decided to go to buy that ice cream. I didn't meet anyone or accomplish anything significant with that purchase, but it was really big for me. It made me completely change my perspective about the purpose of money and the power that inspiration has to change our lives. The next time I had the urge for something, I just followed it, and that's what took me into meeting the people who would invite me or join me in the great experiences I wanted to have. Something as simple as an ice cream, or going for a walk, or attending to a conference, etc., or whatever you are inspired to do, can change your beliefs and perspective. Do whatever you need to do so that your goal may manifest as a reality in your life.

Now, inspiration won't always take you through what may seem a clear and direct path to your goals, and you won't necessarily notice the link between them when it shows up. It will give you hunches, so that you can meet a person, learn an ability, realize something, find a book, be in the exact place and moment, etc., so that your goal may be possible for you. But you must take action.

Let me give you an example that you can relate to, just to illustrate how the Universe works and needs you to co-create with him through your actions. You may have seen the movie "Harry Potter and the Half Blood Prince". There is a part in which Harry has to get some information in possession of Professor Slughorn, who just refuses to talk about it with him. At some point, it becomes necessary for Harry to know the truth, that's his goal, so he decides to drink the Felix Felicis Potion, a liquid which was supposed to give him good luck. After he drank it, he started to feel very good, and had a hunch to go see Hagrid, which was seemingly unrelated to what his goal was. Nevertheless, it just happened that on his way to finding Hagrid, he found Professor Slughorn, who kept him company and at the end, without having Harry to make any effort, but taking action, told him what he wanted to know; he achieved his goal by following what he felt, that hunch.

Therefore, we must pay attention to what our inner voice tells us, because that's the Universe or Divinity in us, who knows what our goals are and the best way to accomplish them. It's not about following our dreams, because we just don't know how. It's about following inspiration, also on the simple things and mainly maybe, what will lead us to our goals.

So, now that you know that something very simple could change your life and become the Midas Touch for you, would take action and let a single ice cream turn your life into gold?

Ricardo Torres was born in Mexico City in 1986. Studied at the Faculty of Law of the Universidad Nacional Autónoma de México (National Autonomous University of Mexico). He worked in the Supreme Court of Justice for five years in the constitutional area, and one more in the event planning business.

3 Miracles
Diana Wakefield

You can hit rock bottom, and in all the misery an opportunity appears that can change the direction of your whole life. This is how my journey with the Law of Attraction (LOA) began. I was a distributor for a NWM, Network Marketing, company and had just taken all the money I had and I used it to attend a conference. I did this on advice of my upline. At the conference, my upline left unexpectedly.

I was so devastated. I found myself alone, broke, and scared. This was not the first time I had faced disaster, but it felt like it was by far the worst. I was sitting in the conference and it was like I was in a movie when there is a lot of noise and activity, but the camera zooms in on me and my thoughts. Only my thoughts of devastation, and this awareness of my body feeling like it was going to explode, existed.

Then everything quieted down inside me and my mind went blank. When thoughts returned, I decided to end my life. Then, in the next second I felt a nudge to stand up and leave, so I stood up and turned around and almost ran into this gentleman standing there. He smiled and started talking to me. I could barely understand him – not only because of his Venezuelan accent, but because

I felt like I was in a bubble and everything around me was turned down. Slowly the bubble dissolved as we talked. He started telling me about how I can be, do or have anything.

I liked what I was hearing, and we continued to talk for hours. After I got home, we stayed in touch and one day I told him where I was mentally and emotionally that day we met. He told me that day he had gone in the wrong doors to the conference. He walked in and did not know where he was and then I stood up. We both agree the Divine brought us together, and this guy with the big smile, George Ruiz, began to mentor me. George told me about the movie "The Secret" and I began to study everyone from The Secret and the LOA .

I was not very successful in the NWM company I was in, and NWM companies were popping up everywhere. I ended up joining thirteen companies and nothing was happening. I knew from the LOA that if I was on the right path it should be much easier than this. So I told the Divine, "I cannot figure it out so you need show me which company I should be working with." I meant a company I was currently in.

A few days later, a client and my sister told me about a lecture by a naturopathic doctor. It was for a NWM company but I was not interested in a fourteenth company, so I told them I could not go because I had two clients booked that night. Then to my surprise, both of my clients called to reschedule, so my evening was free. I knew this was no coincidence. I was supposed to go. I was so excited about this company I signed up right away. Then I signed up my family and I started telling everybody. My business began to grow so rapidly, I got a Rapid Rank Advancement Award (which I did not even know about until I got to the convention and they called me up on stage). It was effortless. If I was so set on it having to be one of the thirteen companies I was already in, I would have missed the opportunity.

Three years later I was doing well, but things started to slow down. I started to feel stress and hard work setting in. I told the Divine I would do whatever it takes, but it was time to make a big change. There was no reason the LOA should not be working for me. I got the feeling I was missing something. I realized one day that I was surrounded by negativity, and that is when it hit me. I would have to connect with positive people who could inspire me.

A few days went by, I was online deleting emails. Just before I clicked delete on an email, something in my gut told me to look at it. I followed the links, which led me to a page offering a group coaching session. I had never considered coaching. But I got nudged to do it, so I did. WOW!!!

That one group coaching session was so powerful, I signed up for Miracles Coaching that day. From there I was inspired to write this chapter. What an incredible opportunity, and I would have never gotten here if I did not listen to that nudge inside. It was effortless once I got on the right track. Once you trust that where you are going is the best design for you, then everything unfolds perfectly. I thought if I let the Divine choose, I would have to give up everything and start over, but my whole life is what led to now, and my future involves sharing my whole life to empower the lives of others through MierCore™ NWM and LOA Coaching.

Diana coaches MierCore™ NWM and LOA Coaching. She can be reached at www.miercore.com - Miracles through Internal Energy Rediscovery is Core to success. Meaning everything is energy and to rediscover that energy and understand how the universe works is key to creating success.

Diana was always meant to be a student and teacher, and first recognized this during college in her twenties. She is most excited and inspired when sharing what she has learned to help benefit the lives of others. Diana's credentials include BS in Psychology, Licensed Massage Therapist, Reiki Master, Personal Trainer, and Network Marketing Coach. Her new found passion is the Law of Attraction (LOA) and helping people rediscover their inner power to achieve success.

Your Soul Purpose IS Your Sole Purpose
Bob Wakitsch

Bangkok, 1955.

Workers are moving a huge concrete Buddha into a new temple. Ropes break and the statue smashes to the ground. Nervous workers inspect the damage and notice a gleaming inside.

Cement is carefully chiseled to uncover a 10 foot, 6 ton deity of solid gold.

Why plaster over solid gold?

The masonry occurred to prevent it from being stolen. As Burmese soldiers overtook the kingdom in 1767, Buddhist monks feared the statue would be confiscated. Quickly, they mixed cement and coated it. Post-invasion, the idol remained among the ruins.

In the early 1800's, the Thai King decreed all Buddha images to be collected from ransacked temples and delivered to Bangkok. This supposedly worthless statue graced several temples until its discovery in 1955.

"In U.S. currency, the gold alone exceeds $250 million dollars making this the most valuable Buddha statue in existence."

As the monks were slaughtered in the invasion, this Buddha's true identity remained hidden for two centuries.

Incredible, isn't it? A priceless artifact concealed within relatively cheap material.

Yet, the same thing is occurring with you. You also have a priceless true identity hidden within a cheap outer suit.

A Soul inhabits every human body. Your Soul is your True Identity. Your Soul is the bridge between the physical universe and the realm of the Divine. You have a foot in both worlds; a connection to each.

Unknown to most, there are four categories of Souls. Each category paves a separate path. Each of the four paths is represented by a different color. Your Soul is one of those colors and designates which path YOU are on.

White is the Path of Peace. Green is of Mercy. Purple is of Truth. Blue is of Love.

Whichever Path you occupy, you're on it for this lifetime. No matter which direction you metaphorically step, your Path appears beneath your feet.

Hence, you can never be lost. You can "imagine" yourself confused, worried, doubtful, or victimized, but those are only illusions. Your Soul is never lost. You're always in the exact, perfect place.

Joy is derived from acting in alignment with your Path.

Suffering is caused by acting in opposition with your Path.

You're also blessed with a specific Soul Quality.

Your Soul Quality IS your life's purpose.

Gurus proclaim your life purpose is something you choose, based upon your loves and talents. Logical, but misleading. Your Soul Purpose *is* your choice, but you chose it with The Divine pre-incarnation. You possess this specific Soul Quality, which places you on a predetermined Path. You experience everything through that identity.

Your Soul Quality is one of the sacred attributes of The Divine.

God and your Soul (your individual aspect of God) decided which Divine Quality you would inherit. Each Quality emits one of the four colors, placing you on that particular Path.

Your purpose is to BE that specific Quality of The Divine, and let it radiate from your heart, no matter your occupation. By BEING your True Identity, you are releasing into the world the grace and gifts your particular Quality carries.

Consequently, you are a uniquely magnificent expression of God radiating in physicality.

Sadly, like the Golden Buddha, most people's True Identity (Soul Quality) remains buried their entire lives, lost to the world.

I know of two ways to identify your Soul Path and Quality:

The first: you feel Joy. Alignment with your Path and Quality immerses you in Joy. Joy means you are vibrating your true essence through your thoughts, words, and actions. While in Joy, you may be able to discern your Soul's purpose. (Conversely, when you feel anything less than Joy, you are denying your Path.)

The second: by contacting me. I have been blessed with a Divine Gift to SEE Soul Colors and Soul Qualities...literally. Instantly upon connecting with your energy, I can visibly see your Soul Color and your Path. Shortly thereafter, I can ascertain your specific Soul Quality.

Essentially, I see God-in-Disguise everywhere, including inside of YOU.

While given this ability at birth, I denied it for almost 50 years. At age 8, my second grade nun condemned me to hell for colluding with the devil. Terrified, I ignored them and the colors eventually disappeared. Forty years later, an enlightened Sufi Master from Jerusalem reawakened them. Frightened again, I ignored them until the death of my 22 year old son in 2011. Reluctantly, I embraced my gift upon realizing I was sabotaging my Divine destiny.

My Soul Quality is Batin Hakim ("Hidden Wisdom"). I'm

endowed with a purpose of revealing to others their own Soul's gift so they may embrace it to live a relevant life.

Souls are our Sources of fulfillment. I've developed several processes called Soul So(u)rcery, allowing you to manifest miracles through your Divinity.

No greater thrill exists than to know with certainty why you're here. You are endowed with a specific purpose; to BE your Soul Quality and dispense it to the world so others can experience Love, Mercy, Peace or Truth through you.

Famed choreographer Martha Graham explained it perfectly to a professional dancer pupil:

"There is a vitality, a life force, an energy, a quickening that is translated through you into action, and because there is only one of you in all of time, this expression is unique. And if you block it, it will never exist through any other medium and it will be lost. The world will not have it. It is not your business to determine how good it is nor how valuable nor how it compares with other expressions. It is your business to keep it yours clearly and directly, to keep the channel open. You do not even have to believe in yourself or your work. You have to keep yourself open and aware to the urges that motivate you."

You ARE a Golden Buddha, yet infinitely more priceless.

God sent you here on a quest. Bob Wakitsch has been entrusted with the Divine gift of KNOWING your True Sacred Identity and how to succeed on your journey. Bob helps seekers embrace their Soul Quality, transcend obstacles and live a life of joy and fulfillment. Go to http://www. truesacredidentity.com now.

Healing Power Within
Mireya Wessolossky

S usan has been sick for the past seven years with what has been diagnosed as "chronic Lyme disease." Her main complaint is chronic fatigue and body aches. She has been treated for Lyme disease many times, despite multiple tests reporting negative for this bacteria. She has visited different doctors, who have prescribed courses of antibiotics for weeks, with marginal response.

Fatigue has made her quit her job and made it impossible to care for her family. She is depressed, hopeless, and despaired.

As I walk into the exam room I hear "*Please, help me*" loud and clear from her soul.

I recognized her suffering, as I do with many others who walk into my office. I looked deep in her eyes wondering if I can talk to her Being.

I dared.

I said to her: "Susan, I have good news and bad news.

The good news... first, you are not going to die from this, and second, you are going to get better.

The bad news... I am not sure when you'll feel better, and second, I have no pills for you to take today. But I know that if you listen to your body and hear what it's telling you, you will get better. If you meditate, do yoga, or Tai Chi, or walk mindfully, it would help you enormously, but more important, connect to your self, your Being and you will feel awesome."

She looked at me like a deer in the middle of the night, illuminated by hunter's flashlight, just before the shot.

The connection between body, mind, and soul is something well recognized as strong, real, and firm. In the medical profession, how we have allowed the separation of what is so connected and intertwined? We treat the body without also treating the mind and the soul.

The wonder of the harmony of the mind, soul and body should be a mandatory subject in medical school. We need to teach the healing power of meditation, yoga, mindfulness, and the Law of Attraction.

We need to empower all our patients with this knowledge, because body, mind and soul are inseparable, powerful and miraculous.

As much scientific and dogmatic as our careers have become, there is evidence of the power of healing we all have, and we all have succumb in the illusion and Ego stage that we (doctors) heal, that we have the power of knowing and healing others.

We all have been seduced by the Ego to have the higher power of healing, but I recognize now that a better approach is helping patients in the awareness of their healing power for a much transformative experience.

Disease is a consequence of unbalance mind-body-soul.

We have the power to stop the suffering of our patients and engage them in a more sustainable, natural, and satisfactory experience in healing.

Let's feed healing and starve dis-ease, starve dis-connection

207

to our divinity, our self, and our being. Let's ask our patient to see themselves healing, strong, and productive. Let's help them regained their life with joy, peace, and love.

Doctors are plagued with the time constraints and regulations imposed on us by health insurance companies and then government, making us disconnected from what our patient really needs. We are sinking our careers just as the Titanic sunk in the middle of the Atlantic. We can claim our lifeboats by teaching the principle of mind, body, and soul in all our medical school.

Let's stop pleasing the status quo that has flatly failed healing our society – just look at the prevalence of diabetes, obesity, drug addiction, cancer, autoimmune disorders, and other maladies. It has contributed enormously in other aspects without a doubt, like vaccinations, antibiotics, surgeries, radiation therapy, et, but there is more in us too that has been neglected or forgotten.

We, as humans, are collectively sick from ignoring the awareness of our own healing powers. But we can gain our health by allowing our patients, and ourselves, to connect with the divine.

Let's stop concentrating on the illness and focus more in the health. As we pay more attention in the illness, that is what we attract, more illness.

As physicians we can ask better questions. Why is this patient attracting this illness? Why this patient is suffering and expressing this illness with the body? What is their body telling us?

Health is an expression of harmony. Sickness is an expression of undone issues that need to be resolved.

There are many ways to connect with the soul. We know, as doctors, that the body heals, repairs, reconnects, and has plasticity. But we have played with fire by ignoring these self-healing powers and jumping into pills, antibiotics, and surgeries. We have neglected the core of our profession by ignoring the connection of the mind, body, and soul.

We owe it to ourselves, to our patients, and our divine profession, to change our practice for a much healthy and truthful path. I am invoking my own strength to be part of these changes.

I hope to serve and educate many of my peers and patients about these principles and act according to them with compassion, joy, love, and peace. We need to start with ourselves, by emphasizing a curriculum that reflects this in our medical training, as soon as a medical student walks into our classroom.

Susan, like many others, was accustomed to the allopathic medicine. So recognizing the strength of connecting to the Being or Self was a foreign land. However, a huge wave is being awakened and spreading rapidly around the globe.

I sense this as a new awakening to return to the nature, to the basics of our own healing powers. I am so happy and thankful now that I am trying to ride this wave with many new health providers. The new generation of medical students seems open and sensitive to their core values, to health. Hopefully, they'll save our broken health system and restore complete health to our patients.

Dr Mireya Wessolossky was born and raised in Caracas-Venezuela. Married with a daughter, she's an infectious diseases specialist with a passion for working with HIV/AIDS. Over the past few years of treating patients and teaching, her focus has shifted to holistic medicine with implementation and concentration in wellness.

Dying...to Get Well

Gloria J. Yorke

My husband, Anthony Dick Sarlo, collapsed at our home in July 2012. He was a Chicago legend, for over 60 years, as an Entertainer, Big Band Orchestra Leader, Singer, and Virtuoso of the Tenor Sax. His repertoire included working with Frank Sinatra, Dean Martin, Sammy Davis, Tony Bennett, Johnny Cash, Mel Torme, and Wayne Newton...among many other known entertainers. As General Manger of the Chicago Pick Congress Hotel, he generated record- breaking revenue that was never duplicated. Additionally, Anthony Dick was a Veteran of World War II, serving as Corporal in the U.S. Marine Corps, and playing in the Halls of Montezuma Band.

The course of events that followed as a result of that fall was the beginning of his end.

From a healthy active senior, he would spiral into a coma, which was caused by doctor error!

The Journal of Patient Safety states that medical "mistakes" contribute to deaths of some 440,000 patients each year!

Thus, with blood all over his brain (Brain Hemorrhage,) the hospital doctor who was assigned to him prescribed a sleeping pill at bedtime, even though I verbally expressed my disagreement with her decision.

During that night he lapsed into a coma, and remained in that state for over a month.

These shocking set of circumstances, catapulted me immediately into a quantum leap as his MEDICAL ADVOCATE, and I was not prepared. I had no medical experience or knowledge. Even the thought of walking into a hospital, and seeing needles and tubes, terrified me. In short, I would have been the last person you would choose to be your Medical Advocate.

Dr. Joe Vitale reminds us that the Law of Attraction (LOA) teaches us to follow our intuition, and that the Universe likes speed. Don't delay or second guess yourself. When the challenge or opportunity arises... take action!

After 2 weeks of being in a coma, the Chief Neurologist examined all of Anthony Dick's test results, and in not being able to ascertain the reason that he was in a coma state, his recommendation to me was, "Let him die!"

My only response to him was, "Apparently, you have never loved anyone!"

My deep burning love for Anthony Dick, overshadowed and diluted all of my fears. I became a completely different person, who was resolute in making him well again, and there was no way I would be deterred.

I became like a lion defending her cub, and came out of the gate at rapid speed. My senses became keen, in watching every single thing that was happening, with much scrutiny. I questioned every administration of medicine, and stayed by his side for 12 hours every day.

He was my entire world, and I was not going to listen to any lame excuses as to why he was in the coma, nor why I should give up on him.

Anthony Dick's immediate family was deceased, and my family lives in Pennsylvania. We had a nucleus of friends, who gave support through calls and emails; but when it came to the day-to-day decision making, I stood alone. Obviously, I depended solely on God, my universe, to give me guidance and direction.

LOA – DEFYING LOGIC

It is extremely important for you to know and remember, that the Universe has unlimited power, and an overabundance of resources. There is never a lack. There is never a wish or dream that cannot be fulfilled. There is only one requirement: BELIEVE!

GUIDELINES FOR BEING A MEDICAL ADVOCATE

LESSON #1 – TRUST YOUR INTUITION. First and foremost. If you feel something is not right, and is NOT in the best interest of the patient, speak up! You know the patient better than the medical staff does... so stand tall, and stand firm. Be adamant, but be respectful, if you disagree.
LOA – DECISIVENESS

LESSON #2 – DON'T BE INTIMIDATED. Your loved one is a human being. Make sure that he or she is shown the proper respect and dignity. If you see otherwise, report it to the Floor Supervisor.
LOA – RESPECT FOR HUMANITY

LESSON #3 – DO RESEARCH. Whatever the illness, information is available for your knowledge on the Internet, library, or bookstore. Do your homework, and be aware of what to look for, such as allergic reactions. This will also aid you in asking intelligent questions to the medical staff.
LOA – SEEK AND YE SHALL FIND

LESSON # 4 – BE OBSERVANT. Read all materials posted in

the room. Always check to see what is being administered for allergic reactions, rashes, diarrhea, nervousness, itching. If you notice any of these things, report it immediately. Everyone should carry a list of their medications with them, especially seniors. Include frequency taken, dosage, doctor's name, allergies, and recent testing.
LOA – ALERTNESS

LESSON # 5 – MAKE YOUR PRESENCE KNOWN. Get to know the doctors and nurses, so they learn for whom you are an Advocate. Believe me… those patients who have a visible advocate get better attention. Meet with them in person. Let them know you understand the illness, and ask what steps will be taken toward a cure.
LOA – I AM

LESSON # 6 – DOCTOR COMMITMENT. If you feel the doctor is not committed to your loved one, and ignores your request to meet with you, then ask for another doctor. There is absolutely no reason for you to be left in the dark, with unanswered questions. Have zero tolerance.
LOA – DUTY

LESSON # 7 – CLEANLINESS. Check everywhere and everything for sanitation. Mark the sheets in a hidden spot if you feel they are not being changed daily, for example. Germs are your major enemy.
LOA – UNIVERSAL HEALTH

LESSON #8 – RESTRICT VISITORS. Prepare a schedule for all family members to visit. This will prevent overwhelming the patient with multiple visitors. Friends can be informed about progress, through phone calls or email.
LOA – RESTRICTIONS

LESSON # 9 – TAKE A BREAK. Yes, Advocate, even you need

a brief separation. Take an entire day off, once a week, and have someone cover for you.

LOA – MANIFEST WELLNESS

LESSON # 10 – BE A POLITICIAN. Comfort your loved one, using only "positive" words. No negatives. Remember the Law of Attraction…. what you say, feel, and visualize, you attract.

As music is a universal medicine, play their favorite CDs, tapes, or records.

Compliment the Medical staff, and bring them cookies or candy.

LOA – UNCONDITIONAL LOVE

Gloria J. Yorke, distinguished Chicago Author, Writer, and Journalist. Master Channeler and communicator to the spiritual realm. Dedicated scholar of the Metaphysical/ Law of Attraction mysticism. Renown Hotel and Resort Director of Sales and Marketing for 30 years. Born and raised in Canonsburg, Pennsylvania. Connect with her at sundance164@gmail.com